THE BIRTH OF ELECTRONIC PUBLISHING

Legal and Economic Issues
in Telephone, Cable and
Over-the-Air Teletext
and Videotext

by
Richard M. Neustadt

Knowledge Industry Publications, Inc.
White Plains, NY and London

Communications Library

Birth of Electronic Publishing: Legal and Economic Issues in Telephone, Cable and Over-the-Air Teletext and Videotext

by Richard M. Neustadt

Library of Congress Cataloging in Publication Data

Neustadt, Richard M.
  Birth of electronic publishing.

  (Communications library)
  Bibliography: p.
  Includes index.
  1. Electronics in printing.   2.   Publishers and
publishing.   I.   Title   II.   Series
  Z249.3.N43   384   82-6614
  ISBN 0-86729-030-7   AACR2

Printed in the United States of America

10   9   8   7   6   5   4   3   2   1

Table of Contents

i

List of Tables and Figures

List of Illustrations

Acknowledgements

Portions of this book are based on an article that appeared in the *Federal Communications Law Journal* in December 1981. That article was co-authored by Richard M. Neustadt, Gregg P. Skall and Michael Hammer. The opinions in this book do not necessarily express the views of Mr. Skall or Mr. Hammer.

Abbe Lowell co-authored the chapter on obscenity and defamation. He is with the Washington, DC law firm of Venable, Baetjer, Howard & Civiletti.

Mr. Neustadt, with the Washington, DC law firm of Kirkland & Ellis, represents several clients involved in electronic publishing, including the Telidon (Canadian) technology and the American Newspaper Publishers Association (ANPA).

The publisher would like to thank the Association of Viewdata Information Providers (AVIP), for permission to reprint portions of its Code of Practice. Copies of the Code are available from AVIP, 102-108 Clerkenwell Rd., London, England EC1M 5SA.

1

Introduction

A new mass medium is emerging in America. Until recently, mass distribution of information has been dominated by publishing and broadcasting. Now, technology is marrying these media to spawn a new one: electronic publishing. Print-type information—text and graphics— is being distributed over electronic channels: television, radio, cable TV and telephone wires. In the past four years, electronic publishing has changed from futuristic fantasy into a serious business. In time, this technology may change the way we create, obtain and use information.

This marriage unites vastly different traditions. Publishing and broadcasting have different technologies, economic structures and styles, and they are governed by different laws and regulations. In print, anyone can publish, and government control is limited to rules on obscenity and defamation. Broadcasters, in contrast, need government permission to go on the air, and the government has developed detailed regulations on content, access, rates and ownership.

Electronic publishing, however, has no place in the law at present. No statute or regulation mentions it, and the first court decision on this medium was issued in the fall of 1981. In the next few years, policy-makers must answer a string of questions to fill this vacuum. How will the First Amendment apply—will electronic publishers have the full freedom of newspapers or will they be covered by content regulations, as are broadcasters? Will would-be electronic publishers have access to the electronic channels of communication—is regulation needed to ensure diversity and competition? Should the government set technical stan- dards to make systems compatible or should it leave that issue to the marketplace? Are privacy policies needed to protect consumers from misuse of the vast data banks the new technologies will create? Does current copyright law adequately protect the investments of those who create the information?

1

These kinds of issues have been debated passionately in the print and broadcast contexts for 50 years and the answers for this new medium will illuminate and may alter that old debate. This book was written to help start the new discussion. Many of the issues are legal, but the book is also intended for non-lawyers. All the businesses now probing at the edges of electronic publishing—newspapers, telephone companies, cable companies, book publishers and others—have a stake in how the laws are written. They must understand the rules of the game if they are to play it profitably. Moreover, everyone else will be affected by these decisions. If electronic publishing becomes a powerful and pervasive information medium, the decisions being made now will have an important impact on the kind of society we live in at the end of the century. The policies to be made in the next few years are likely to last a long time.

In each area covered, this book briefly explains the laws and rules now in place and then discusses how these regulations will affect electronic publishing. The book goes on to suggest what the new policies should be and how regulators, legislators and judges can implement those policies.

The book begins with an outline of the technology of electronic publishing and the kinds of marketing applications now being developed. The next section (Chapters 3 through 7) deals with the traditional issues of communications policy: Chapter 3 outlines the Communications Act; Chapter 4 discusses how the Act's policies should apply to electronic publishing; and Chapters 5 through 7 deal with specific application to over-the-air, telephone and cable TV transmission.

Chapter 8 outlines the current debate about whether the FCC should set a technical standard for over-the-air services. Chapter 9 deals with the threat to personal privacy from the maintenance of massive data bases containing detailed information on what people read, what they buy, what they watch, and so on. Chapter 10 covers defamation and obscenity—issues that all publishers must consider. Chapter 11 explains the copyright protections available to electronic publishers and describes novel copyright problems posed by this technology. Chapter 12 sets out a proposal for an overall policy for electronic publishing. Finally, since videotext has a longer history in Britain, we thought it worthwhile to include excerpts from the Association of Viewdata Information Providers' "Code of Practice" in an Appendix at the end of the book.

The business of electronic publishing is so new that it is hard to be confident about the "right" answers. That is one reason many of the policies suggested here involve minimum government intervention and maximum freedom to experiment. In any case, these answers are offered with great modesty. If they help focus attention on the questions, this book will have achieved its purpose.

NOTE FOR READERS

The following is intended to aid readers who may be unaccustomed to legal citations:

1. Federal laws are cited with the volume number (called "title" by lawyers), followed by the abbreviation U.S.C. (meaning United States Code), followed by the particular section. For example, 47 U.S.C. 315 means Section 315 of Title 47 of the U.S. Code.

2. Federal regulations are cited with the volume, followed by C.F.R. (meaning Code of Federal Regulations), followed by the section number (e.g., 47 C.F.R. 78).

3. Court cases are cited with the name of the case, followed by the volume number of the book that reports the case, followed by a symbol indicating which kind of court decided the case, followed by the page number and the date the case was decided. Except for the Supreme Court, these codes also include the name of the court, just before the date. Thus, *Harris v. Jones*, 318 F.2d 431 (3d. Cir., 1978) means the case is printed in volume 318 of the Second Series of the Federal Reporter at page 431, and that it was decided by the U.S. Court of Appeals for the Third Circuit.

2

How Electronic Publishing Works

The concept of electronic publishing is simple: pages of text and graphics are displayed on a television set or other inexpensive screen. The technology is cheap and easy enough to use that it may become a mass medium. It can give people information they now get from newspapers, magazines and books—quickly, conveniently and with access to vast information resources.

This industry is in its infancy, but afficionados are already debating its semantics. There are passionate arguments over the meaning and even the spelling of basic terms. In this book, "teletext" means a one-way system, with signals flowing to the user. In a typical teletext system, a single set of electronic pages is beamed simultaneously to all users. The pages are on a cycle that repeats every few seconds. The user has a terminal attached to a television set; by using the keyboard, the user instructs the terminal to "grab" a page from the cycle. The page is displayed on the screen until the user calls for the next one.

"Videotext" is two-way. The computer holds a large number of pages (a data base), and the user sends a signal to it to request the desired page. The computer then transmits that particular page. Videotext sends different pages to different users and can handle multiple requests simultaneously. In basic terms, teletext works like television and videotext works like the telephone.

THE DEVELOPMENT OF ELECTRONIC PUBLISHING

Forms of electronic publishing have been in use for several years. Many cable television systems devote one channel to a continuous "scroll" of news and weather—a primitive kind of teletext. Data base searching systems are a form of videotext, and their use by libraries, scientists, businesses and law firms for research is expanding rapidly. The current breakthrough is that technological advances, declining costs and marketing initiatives are making electronic publishing a mass medium. Market tests have been underway for several years, and Britain started full-scale commercial services two years ago. Commercial services are scheduled to begin in the United States in 1982.

One reason for this growth is convenience. Electronic publishing offers users access to a vast library of information. Distance is no longer a barrier—users in small towns can dial up data bases anywhere. Time also can be conquered—electronic publishers can update their data bases as often as they want.

Another driving force is economics. Electronic publishing replaces paper, printing and physical delivery or postage—all of which are rapidly getting more expensive. Cable TV entrepreneur Ted Turner has described the economics graphically:

> There's nothing more inefficient than going out and chopping down trees that we're going to need for firewood and making them into paper and printing the damn paper every day. And then, with oil supplies drying up, driving them all over town and sticking those bulky things in everybody's mailbox. And then we have to send the garbage trucks to pick them up.[1]

The costs of electronics are quite different. The costs of computer memory and processing are falling at about 15% per year. Local telephone transmission rates are rising, but less rapidly than inflation over the long term. Other transmission rates are stable or falling. (See Figure 2.1.) One reason for electronics' advantage is continuing technological progress. Another is the fact that communications is not dependent on scarce natural resources; the entire U.S. phone system is powered for a year on the energy carried by one oil tanker.

The increasing use of computers in business and schools also will benefit electronic publishing for, as Americans become more comfortable with computers, they will be more likely to bring them home. Finally, electronic home banking and home shopping are expected to speed rapidly as the cost of maintaining physical bank and retail outlets escalates. Those services require videotext terminals, and their expansion also should help bring electronic publishing into the home.

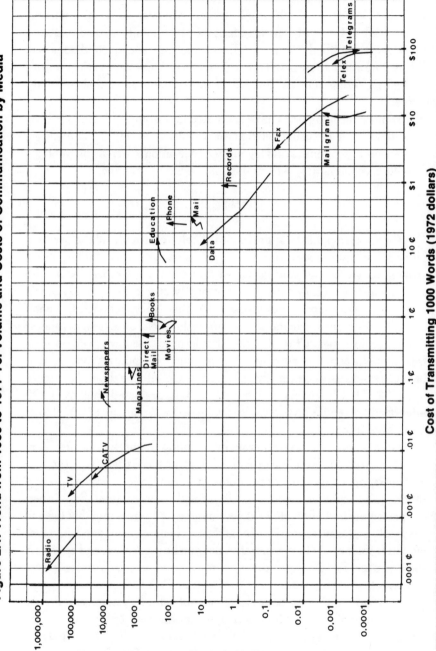

Figure 2.1: Trend from 1960 to 1977-78: Volume and Costs of Communication by Media

Source: Reprinted with permission from the M.I.T. Research Program on Communications Policy, Fifth Report, September 1981.

In spite of these trends, the growth rate of electronic publishing is hard to predict. Some thought electronic delivery of newspapers was imminent in 1938, when the newly invented facsimile technology offered what one eager writer dubbed "readio."[2] Economic and social conditions are different now, but there is still no evidence that Americans are clamoring to read flickering screens, instead of newspapers, over their morning coffee.

Various consulting firms have estimated that from 7% to 25% of U.S. households will be using teletext or videotext in 1990. Thereafter, convenience, economics and a younger generation's increasing familiarity with computers may well make this medium pervasive.

CONTENT

As electronic publishing grows, it is likely to provide all the services offered by newspapers—news, sports, weather, stock tables, horoscopes, movie listings and classified and display advertisements. The systems also will carry some kinds of highly current or special interest information not found in newspapers, such as airline schedules, reports on traffic conditions, telephone directories, financial analyses, consumer reports and recipes. Classified ads should do particularly well on electronic publishing, because the content can be updated quickly and because home users can easily call up the page with the desired category (e.g., "1978 Chevrolets"). One expert has predicted that by 1990 advertising revenues on teletext and videotext will represent 10% of total U.S. advertising.

System operators may generate information themselves or may contract for it with "information providers" such as advertisers, wire services and newspapers. Revenues may come from subscribers, advertisers and others (e.g., airlines) who wish to provide information. Subscriber-supported teletext and videotext services may charge a monthly fee and may sell or lease terminals. In addition, because videotext involves signals from the user to the operator, use can be measured, and operators may charge for the time the system is used and/or for the pages requested.

In addition to information, electronic publishing systems can handle "electronic mail." Individual messages can be sent by videotext, and "addressed" messages are possible for teletext — the latter would be recorded by terminals programmed to pick out individual items from a stream of radio messages.

Prestel's videotext system allows users to send personalized messages. Courtesy Prestel.

Finally, as mentioned, videotext can handle transactions. Systems are being developed to let consumers browse through electronic catalogues, order goods and services and pay bills through the keyboard on home terminals.

TECHNOLOGY

Most teletext and videotext systems are digital, although broadcast and cable TV systems transmit some text services on an analog basis.

Most systems designed for the United States put 20 lines of 40 spaces each on an "electronic page." Thus a page can hold up to 800 characters (including spaces), or about 150 words. Most pages in current tests include graphics and blank space to make the information easy and attractive to read, so a typical page has about 80 words. (This compares with about 400 words on this page and about 3000 words on the front page of a newspaper.)

In teletext, the number of pages in the system depends on the speed that the cycle is moving past the terminal and on the user's willingness to wait for a page to come around after it is requested. Speed depends on the capacity of the transmission medium. Transmission may be "broadband" (high capacity, such as a full TV channel, which can carry millions of bits per second) or "narrowband" (limited capacity, with a few thousand bits per second). As for delay, most designers believe the average wait should be no more than three or four seconds, making the entire cycle six to eight seconds long.

Teletext waiting time can be reduced and the number of pages increased by building extra memory into the terminal to "grab" several pages at a time. Because the cost of memory is declining and some transmission costs are rising, some entrepreneurs are developing information distribution systems that broadcast electronic newsletters and electronic mail at night, to be received and stored in small computers for access the next morning.

Teletext Technology Options

Teletext can use four media, each with its own potential capacity:

Television

Broadband (full channel) service is possible, and at least one station is

With teleshopping, the video shopper can choose from among several categories of merchandise.

Video advertisements provide shoppers with the information they need and the convenience of shopping at home. Courtesy Telidon.

experimenting with such a text service, for broadcast late at night after regular programming ends. (This service operates like regular TV, broadcasting one page at a time, so it does not require a terminal.) If demand is high and if the FCC grants permission, teletext eventually might become a full channel service on many UHF TV stations. Full channel teletext can provide 5000 or more pages.

For the next few years, however, the main television teletext service will be narrowband and will be transmitted on the vertical blanking interval (VBI). The VBI is the time used when the scanner that produces the TV signal returns from the bottom of the picture to the top. It appears as a dark line when the picture is rolled vertically. The VBI has 21 of the 525 picture lines on U.S. TV sets. Current VBI teletext tests use 2 to 4 lines, providing 80 to 150 pages. By 1990, 11 lines will be available for teletext, and each station will be able to broadcast over 500 pages. (TV stations also may be able to transmit teletext over a portion of their audio signals, although no such systems are being developed at present.)

In addition to existing television stations, broadband and narrowband teletext may be transmitted on two future services: low power TV and Direct-Satellite-to-home Broadcasting. The FCC has proposed the first as a way to create new stations in the coverage gaps between regular stations. Low power TV may provide several hundred new stations, with coverage of 500 to 1200 square miles each. DBS involves TV signals bounced off satellites and received by small, rooftop antennas. Depending on FCC and international decisions, DBS may provide several dozen nationwide TV channels by 1986.

Radio

FM stations can use a portion of their frequencies (the "subcarrier") to transmit narrowband teletext, without interfering with the regular signal. Each station can broadcast several hundred teletext pages. The information is distributed in the same manner as VBI teletext, i.e., a digital data stream. The subscriber connects his radio receiver to a television set or computer to display the information.

Multipoint Distribution Service (MDS)

MDS is an over-the-air service that uses microwave frequencies— requiring a special antenna—to transmit pay television or data. MDS may provide full channel or VBI teletext. To the user, teletext on MDS looks the same as on regular television—the only difference is the extra expense of the special antenna.

Cable

Cable television may provide a VBI service on each channel as well as one or more full channels of teletext. Thus, a modern 36-channel cable system with one dedicated teletext channel and VBI services on the others could carry a total of over 10,000 pages. Time Inc. has announced a full channel teletext service for distribution to cable systems thoughout the country.

Videotext Technology Options

Videotext has no technical limit on the size of the data base; a system can hold millions of pages. However, the index gets more complex as the data base gets bigger, and that may make it harder for the user to find a desired page. In addition, the bigger the data base, the more expensive the computer. Videotext can be transmitted either by telephone or cable.

Telephone

The telephone is the leading videotext medium because it is a two-way network that is switchable (i.e., different messages can be routed to different subscribers simultaneously). Telephone transmission is slow— about a fifth of a page a second—but current research is expected to speed it up. AT&T is working on a system that will allow videotext use on one telephone extension while letting regular calls come in on the others. The most significant constraints on the increasing use of telephone videotext are that local rates are likely to rise substantially during the 1980s and that widespread use of videotext would strain the network's current capacity.

Cable

Cable's advantage over the telephone is its greater capacity; each cable channel can handle more than 1000 times as much information as a telephone line, and modern cable systems have from 32 to over 100 channels. A few cable systems are experimenting with two-way services, using a full channel to carry signals "downstream" to the user and another channel or a VBI to carry signals "upstream" to the computer. Cable will only slowly move into such pure videotext services because almost all existing systems are one-way and do not switch; however, cable will be widely used for hybrid services. Typically, the subscriber will use the telephone network to call "upstream" to the computer, and it will send the pages back "downstream" by cable. This approach takes advantage of cable's great capacity to handle the downstream signals, which involve more data than the short "orders" sent upstream. The hybrid approach thereby minimizes transmission charges because it makes only brief use of the telephone network. If hybrid services prove popular, they may also be used with broadcast transmission. The "down-stream" signal would be sent over the air, while the "upstream" message would go by telephone. These transmission options are summarized in Table 2.1.

Table 2.1: Summary of Teletext and Videotext Transmission Options

Capacity	Teletext	Videotext
Narrowband	TV broadcast (VBI) MDS (VBI) Cable (VBI) FM radio (subcarrier) Perhaps low power TV (VBI) and direct broadcast satellite (VBI)	Telephone Hybrid: telephone upstream and VBI or FM subcarrier downstream
Broadband	Cable (full channel) MDS (full channel) Perhaps low power TV and DBS (full channel)	Cable Hybrid: telephone upstream and cable (or MDS) downstream

HARDWARE AND COSTS

To receive teletext or videotext, the user needs a terminal, which may be wired to the text display tube or built in. Terminal costs vary with the features, such as the ability to present detailed and varied page layouts and to store pages for later display. Teletext terminals require only a key pad with a dozen buttons (marked 0-9, "enter" and so on) and a decoder with a small microprocessor, including some electronic memory. Current tests are using specially designed units costing hundreds of dollars, but these costs will decline rapidly when mass production begins. In a few years, teletext terminals are likely to be built into television sets and should add only $25 to $50 to the cost of the set. Videotext terminals usually are more complex and expensive; they may include a full alpha-numeric keyboard and the device (called a "modem") needed to channel digital videotext signals into the analog telephone network. However, simple videotext terminals may cost under $100 when in mass production.

The other important costs to the user are transmission charges and subscription fees. These may range from zero for advertiser-supported teletext to $20 per month or more for telephone access to valuable data bases.

Each electronic publisher needs one or more "information provider systems" to create the electronic pages. These devices can cost $2000 to $15,000 depending on their capacity for graphics, colors and so on. System operators also must buy or lease a computer and other hardware. For a typical broadcast teletext service, the minimum capital investment will be about $100,000. For videotext the investment depends on the number of users and pages; a large system costs $1 million or more, but a small operator could provide a few thousand pages for a few users with a substantially smaller investment. In addition to paying for information, electronic publishers must pay editors to create pages, operators to run machines, and accountants to handle bills. These operating expenses will vary widely, depending on the service's size and information content.

MARKET STRUCTURE

Many of the policy decisions in electronic publishing depend on the vigor of competition. To understand this market, it must be assessed both vertically (tracking each stage from information creation to final distribution) and horizontally (assessing whether electronic publishing is really one market or several).

Vertical Structure

Electronic publishing involves four distinct businesses that differ in capital, skill, marketing requirements and degree of competition: terminal manufacture and distribution, transmission, publishing and content creation.

Terminal Equipment

Terminals may be free standing, built into television sets or combined with telephones. They will vary widely in function and cost, and probably will be available for sale or lease. The terminal market is likely to be highly competitive if electronic publishing proves popular. Key participants should include AT&T (through its Western Electric manufacturing arm), television manufacturers such as RCA, Zenith and Sony, and the manufacturers of personal computers, such as IBM, Apple and Radio Shack.

Transmission

Like other communications media, the potential bottleneck in electronic publishing is in transmission channels; therefore, this is the area in which many of the policy issues arise.

Narrowband teletext can be provided by each television and radio station and by MDS and cable, so a dozen or more companies should be able to provide this service in each large market. For full channel teletext, cable is likely to be the leading medium, but broadcast TV and MDS do offer possible competition.

For videotext, the telephone network currently is the only means of reaching the general public. Cable systems are experimenting with two-way and hybrid services, and the competition for cable franchises is pushing cable operators to provide such systems. However, the cable role is limited at present because only about one household in four subscribes to cable, many existing systems have all their channels committed to other services, and even in heavily cabled areas substantial numbers of people do not subscribe. By mid-decade, cable probably will be offering two-way or hybrid videotext operations in a large number of cities. Eventually, over-the-air services may provide another competing local distribution network for hybrid videotext.

Publishing

The actual "publishing" function includes deciding what content to provide, operating the computers that will hold the "electronic pages" and selling the service to consumers. This part of the business has the potential for considerable diversity.

Each teletext service can have its own publisher, although in some cases numerous teletext outlets would be used to distribute a single, national service. (Time Inc., for example, plans to distribute a broadband service to many cable operators.)

Videotext allows use of the telephone network to reach an unlimited number of electronic publishers, each with its own data base. Many videotext systems, however, will work through "gateways": a gateway operator will acquire the computer and handle the transmission to the home, and as users' requests for information come in, the operator will route them to member companies' bases or to banks or retailers. Some observers expect one or two such gateways to emerge in each market, with entities such as the local newspaper or bank making the investment to establish and promote the system and then taking a profit on each transaction that passes through it. Such gateways also might route subscribers to national data bases, but subscribers are likely to dial up such information directly. The economies of scale that make gateways likely at the local level will be less powerful for national data base publishing.

If the economies of scale in local videotext operations do prove to be high, then the number of electronic publishers in each market will be limited. In that case, an important policy issue will be whether local gateway operators will sign exclusive controls with a few information and transaction providers or will open their data bases to all users.

On the other hand, the economics of electronic publishing tend to "unbundle" the information services that print publishers provide as a package. Users will be able to call up individual pages and subscribe to specialized services without receiving unrequested information. This will tend to decentralize control of information content. Moreover, the investment required to become an electronic publisher is low, compared, for example, to that required to start a daily newspaper or a television station. The technology offers the possibilities of broadening the sources of information and of tailoring information to particular interests.

Content Creation

The last player in electronic publishing is the information provider.

This category includes authors, print publishers who contribute their material and those who design the "electronic pages." The latter activity is a simple process that can be performed by machine if the page is text only; however, if the page requires sophisticated colors and graphics it may require a demanding, creative procedure requiring as much as half an hour from a skilled craftsman.

For now, at least, most of the content of electronic publishing is likely to come from existing sources. Publishers of cookbooks, for example, will sell the electronic publishing rights to an electronic publisher for inclusion in a data base.

Horizontal Structure

Different technologies may lead to the development of several distinct businesses.

- Narrowband teletext over TV and cable is likely to provide free information of interest to mass audiences, such as news, community calendars, theater listings and classified advertisements. Because each system is limited to a small data base, these services seem more likely to be supported by advertisers and other information providers than by subscribers.

- Broadband teletext and videotext may provide financial, research or other high-value information—especially time-sensitive information—for subscribers who pay by the month or—for videotext—by the page. This market seems likely to begin with business users, who may start with installation of terminals in their offices and then add terminals for home use.

- Videotext may be used for transactions such as shopping, banking, and airline tickets and theater reservations. Revenue could come from buyers, sellers or both.

- Videotext may provide "electronic mail." In this incarnation, messages would be sent to individual subscribers. These might be the same kinds of messages now sent by the mails; videotext would provide instantaneous transmission and—eventually— lower cost. With this application, the revenue probably would come from those sending the messages.

Several key policy issues depend on how markets are defined. Teletext and videotext may be considered two markets; or broadband and narrowband teletext may be different markets. The business is too new to do more than speculate.

CURRENT SERVICES AND TESTS

The British Post Office has a generally available videotext service (called "Prestel"); the British Broadcasting Corporation (BBC) is marketing teletext ("Ceefax"); and Britain's independent broadcasting service also has a teletext operation ("Oracle"). Tests with other technologies have also been underway for years in Canada ("Telidon"), France ("Antiope"), Japan ("Captain") and Germany (using a variety of technologies), and widespread marketing in these countries is expected shortly. Table 2.2 lists existing videotext and teletext services throughout the world.

In the United States, the one teletext service widely available today is "closed captioning," which uses the VBI to transmit captions for regular television shows to hearing-impaired viewers. Videotext-type services now available to the general public include "The Source" and "Compuserve," national data bases that can be reached over telephone lines by home computers with alphanumeric terminals.

A few examples illustrate the variety of experiments underway in the United States.

Indax

Cox Cable is testing this videotext system in San Diego (CA) and has included it in franchise commitments in Omaha (NE) and other cities. It uses two dedicated cable channels—one in each direction—to provide information, electronic mail and home banking and shopping.

Viewtron

This videotext system, operating in Coral Gables (FL), transmits information generated by Knight-Ridder Newspapers over AT&T's lines. The project makes 18,000 information pages available to several hundred households. The data bases include news, weather, sports, product ratings and lists of adult education courses, with department stores, a grocery store, a bookshop and a bank participating. Users can

Table 2.2: Videotext and Teletext Services Around the World

Country	Service Name	Start Date	Terminals
NORTH AMERICA			
United States	BISON (Belo Information Systems Online Network)*, Dallas, TX	July 1981	190
	CBS/AT&T Videotex, Ridgewood, NJ	Fall 1982	200
	CompuServe (*Columbus Dispatch*), Columbus, OH	July 1980	23,300
	ConTelevision (Continental Telephone), Manassas, VA	Late 1982	100[1] 500[2]
	Cox Cable INDAX[3]		
	San Diego	1981	300[4]
	Omaha	1981	N.A.
	New Orleans	April 1982	N.A.
	Dow Jones News/Retrieval	1973	39,000
	FirstHand (First Bank Systems, Minneapolis), North Dakota Test	May 1982	250
	KPIX Teletext, San Francisco, CA	June 1982	100[4]
	Los Angeles Teletext Trial (KCET, KNBC, KNXT)	April 1981	100[4]
	The Source (Reader's Digest)	June 1979	14,100[5]
	Time Inc. Video Information Service (teletext)	Fall 1982	400[4]
	Times Mirror Videotex, Palos Verdes and Mission Viejo, CA	March 1982	350
	ViewTimes (*Danbury News-Times*), Danbury, CT (teletext)	Summer 1982	50[4]
	Viewtron (Knight-Ridder/AT&T), Coral Gables, FL	July 1983	5,000
	WETA Teletext, Washington, DC	June 1981	50
	WFLD Keyfax Teletext, Chicago, IL	April 1981	100

Table 2.2: Videotext and Teletext Services (continued)

Country	Service Name	Start Date	Terminals
United States (cont'd.)	WGBH Teletext, Boston, MA	Summer 1982	20[2]
	WKRC Teletext, Cincinnati, OH	March 1982	50
Canada	Canatel (Canadian Government)	April 1981	40; 100[4]
	Grass Roots, Manitoba	1981	380[6]
	Mercury, New Brunswick	1980/81	45
	Novatex (Teleglobe Canada International)	N.A.	50
	Teleguide, Ontario	July 1982	1,200[4]
	Telidon (Alberta Government Telephone)		
	Calgary Library Trial	September 1981[7]	7
	Alberta Educational Trial	January 1982[7]	6
	Saskatchewan Telephone	September 1982	N.A.
	Vista (Bell Canada)	1981	490
EUROPE			
Finland	Telset	1980	310
France	Teletel (Velizy only)	mid-1981	3,000
	Electronic Directory	N.A.	2,000
	Private business projects	N.A.	500
Germany	Bildschirmtext	June 1980	7,500
Hungary	Teletext Test Transmission	1980	N.A.
Italy	Videotel	1st quarter 1982	1,000

Table 2.2: Videotext and Teletext Services (continued)

Country	Service Name	Start Date	Terminals
Netherlands	Viditel	August 1980	5,000
Norway	Teledata	1980	100
Spain	Spanish Videotext Project	1978	200
Sweden	Text-TV (teletext)	1979/1980	35,000[8]
	Teledata (videotext trial)	1979	100[8]
Switzerland	N.A.	November 1979	113
United Kingdom	Prestel	October 1979	16,000
	Teletext	1975	500,000
FAR EAST			
Hong Kong	Viewdata	Spring 1982	500[4]
Japan	Captain	December 1979	2,000
AFRICA			
South Africa	Beltel	1982	300
SOUTH AMERICA			
Brazil	N.A.	1981	2,000
Venezuela	N.A.	1981	30

*Service suspended May 1982.
N.A. Not available
[1]Projected for first six months.
[2]Projected for second six months.
[3]In May 1982, Cox Cable announced a joint venture with ABC Video Enterprises to evaluate and expand existing services.
[4]Projected.
[5]As of January 1982.
[6]30 terminals incorporated from the original Ida trial; 150 are Elie terminals (fiber optic technology).
[7]Ending June 1982.
[8]As of summer 1981.
Source: Compiled by Knowledge Industry Publications, Inc., based on information supplied by system owners, as well as estimates from Arlen Communications Inc.; *Guide to Electronic Publishing: Opportunities in Online and Viewdata Services*, by Fran Spigai and Peter Sommer (White Plains, NY: Knowledge Industry Publications, Inc., 1982); *The Print Publisher in an Electronic World* (White Plains, NY: Knowledge Industry Publications, Inc., 1981) and *Videotex '81* (England: Online Conferences Ltd., 1981).

make airline and theater reservations and read classified advertisements. Based on the initial results, Knight-Ridder has begun signing videotext franchise agreements with other newspapers.

Green Thumb

In Kentucky, farmers are using telephone lines to obtain pages on weather, crop prices and farming conditions. This government-sponsored system uses a "dump and disconnect" mode of operation; it receives a burst of information, stores it in the terminal memory, and then provides retrieval and display when the user requests it. This "intermittently interactive" system minimizes telephone transmission cost and congestion of the telephone network. The initial project began in 1979 and reached 200 homes.

WETA

New York University's Alternate Media Center launched a teletext trial in 1981 using the VBI of Washington DC, public broadcasting station WETA. This service is providing over 100 pages of information on such subjects as public services, health, consumer information, job listings, news, personal messages and entertainment. Terminals have been placed in public buildings such as libraries, bars and hotel lobbies, as well as in homes. Among the information providers are *The Washington Post*, federal agencies and libraries.

Firsthand

First Bank System, Inc. (FBS), Fargo, ND, plans to test a fully transactional system which will include banking and shopping together with information retrieval. Terminals are being placed in customer homes and small businesses in Fargo.

FBS uses the telephone network to provide agribusiness bookkeeping systems, weather, commodity and financial reports and news. Users may also execute financial transactions, select electronic video games or view advertising and order goods.

CBS/AT&T

CBS and AT&T will test videotext in 200 households in Ridgewood, NJ, beginning in the fall of 1982. CBS will be responsible for all the information content and AT&T will provide the transmission facilities.

WFLD-TV

WFLD-TV in Chicago has been broadcasting a conventional 100-page teletext magazine since April 1981, which includes headline news service, classified advertising (automatic help wanted, real estate and merchandise). On September 4, 1981 it inaugurated "Nite Owl," a full channel text service that does not need a decoder. This service operates each morning from midnight to 6 a.m. and provides entertainment and financial information and advertising. The information is packaged into 20-minute cyclems which can be continually updated. In early 1982, Field announced that it would offer its VBI service to cable systems nationwide. The signal will be transmitted in the VBI of "superstation" WTBS.

KNXT-TV

The CBS network began an on-air VBI teletext experiment with an 80-page magazine in April 1981, over its owned and operated KNXT (TV) in Los Angeles. The test includes advertising and captioning components as well as news and community notices.

FOOTNOTES

1. Ted Turner, Speech to the Dallas Advertising League.
2. Alfred Goldsmith, et al., *Radio Facsimile.* New York: RCS Institute Technical Press, 1938, p. 335.

3

Current U.S. Communications Policy

Electronic publishing may perform the functions of newspspers, but its legal status is very different. Because it uses electronic transmission, it is governed by the Communications Act of 1934. That Act, together with state and local laws, regulates the use of over-the-air signals, telephone wires and cable TV. These rules may also control the content of electronic publishing, the prices that subscribers pay and the vigor of competition in this new medium.

THE STRUCTURE OF THE COMMUNICATIONS ACT

The Communications Act—the basic charter of U.S. communications policy—incorporates three distinct regulatory schemes. One portion was written for broadcasting. Congress had radio in mind in 1934, but television comes under the same umbrella. These provisions were written because radio stations had been broadcasting on each others' frequencies, thus creating electronic chaos. Government licensing was seen as necessary to make radio work efficiently and the number of frequencies available was limited, so Congress decided to treat those who received licenses as "public trustees." It instructed the federal regulators to give licenses for limited periods to those who would provide the "best" services. Over the years this concept spawned amendments to the law and FCC regulations to make broadcasting content serve public purposes and to limit concentration of ownership. Congress also reserved power over broadcasting for the federal government; state and local authorities have no role.

Another portion of the Act was written for the telephone industry. Most of these provisions were modeled on a law passed in the late nineteenth century to regulate railroads. Like railroads, telephone companies are viewed as "common carriers"—monopolies obliged to carry messages for anyone who wants to use their services. To prevent abuse of their monopoly power, common carriers' rates and services are regulated, but the content they carry is not. The Act gives federal regulators responsibility for interstate operations, while states control intrastate services. The FCC has also classified telegraph and satellite carriers under the common carrier rubric.

The Act has still another category for nonbroadcast users of radio frequencies. This group includes mobile radios (e.g., radios in taxi cabs), citizens band, the microwave links used by telephone companies, and other services. These users are to be given licenses if they offer useful services, but neither "public trustee" nor rate regulation applies.

To administer all these policies, the Act created a seven-member Federal Communications Commission. The Commissioners serve for seven-year terms, and no more than four may be from any political party. State regulation usually is handled by the public utility commissions that also regulate power companies.

Recent, dramatic advances in communications technology have bent this 48-year-old framework to the breaking point. Cable television is the best example—it does not appear in the Act at all. Cable began as a means of relaying TV signals in hilly terrain, and the FCC imposed "public trustee" and other regulations on the theory that cable is "ancillary" to broadcasting. In the last five years, cable has grown from a stepchild to a unique and powerful medium that performs functions of both broadcasters and common carriers and fits neither regulatory model. Many of the FCC rules were eliminated recently, but local regulation has mushroomed. Cable uses city streets and conduits, so cable operators need local approval ("franchises") to go into business. Local authorities are using this power to impose rules that vary widely from town to town.

MDS is another service that straddles regulatory lines. It is most often used for pay TV, and it looks like television to the viewer. However, the FCC had data transmission in mind when it created this service. The Commission did not want to apply the broadcasting regulations, so it classified MDS as common carriage.

In the broadcast area, the number of radio and TV stations has doubled since 1960. This proliferation—along with the growth of cable and the prospect of low power TV and DBS—has raised serious doubts about the rationale of frequency "scarcity" that has supported "public trustee" regulation. As a result, Congress and the FCC are now cutting back on content and other regulations.

As for the telephone industry, technological advances—such as use of microwaves and satellites to communicate, instead of telephone wires—have reduced economies of scale and made competition feasible. Entrepreneurs have seized these opportunities and pushed the FCC to allow competitive services. During 15 years of battles at the Commission and the courts, the federal rules that maintained AT&T's monopoly were dismantled. With the barriers to entry down, more and more competitors are challenging AT&T in long distance service and in telephone equipment. Even at the local level, cable and over-the-air services are beginning to compete with the telephone companies. As a result, the underpinnings of common carrier regulations are collapsing, and the courts, the FCC and Congress are now developing a different set of rules.

Electronic publishing is being born into a policy world in flux, as old regulatory categories blur into each other. This new service is itself an example of the blurring: it may be provided by broadcasters, common carriers or cable TV. Nevertheless, the principles and mechanisms of the Communications Act remain in effect. Pending legislation may change some provisions, but the basic scheme is likely to remain on the books and to shape this new medium.

POLICY TOOLS

United States communications policy is based on three ideals that often conflict: 1) that communications should be controlled by the private sector, not the government; 2) that communications channels should be affordable, widely available and used in ways that serve the public interest; and 3) that competition should be encouraged, with particular emphasis on diversity in the sources of information. Current regulations use three tools:

- *Content regulation* is supposed to make broadcasters provide public interest programs, give listeners varying viewpoints and exclude offensive material.

- *Rate regulation* is intended to make transmission rates reasonable and nondiscriminatory.

• *Structural regulation* governs entry, ownership and access. It is currently being used to promote diversity and competition.

CONTENT REGULATION

The Communications Act imposes some content controls on broadcasters, and the FCC has used the "public trustee" principle to add to its own policies. Five sets of content rules could have major impacts on electronic publishing:

(a) The Act's political broadcasting rules require licensees to give qualified candidates for federal elective office "reasonable" access to the airwaves—meaning a right to buy advertising time.[1] In addition, if one candidate is given coverage or is sold time, broadcasters must give competing candidates equal opportunities. (This is often called the "Equal Time" rule.) This requirement does not prevent stations from providing regular news coverage of candidates—that is how broadcasters cover elections without being required to give time to all the minor party candidates—but it does apply to advertising and special broadcasts. The Act also requires that air time sold to candidates be at the minimum rate.[2]

(b) The Act requires broadcast licensees to cover controversial issues of public importance and to present opposing points of view on those issues (the "Fairness Doctrine"). If a broadcast contains an attack on the honesty or character of a person or group, FCC rules require the licensee to notify the party and offer a chance to respond. The same rule applies if a broadcast editorial endorses or opposes a political candidate.[3]

(c) FCC guidelines on license renewals impel television broadcasters to originate a certain amount of programming locally, to provide at least a minimum amount of news, public affairs and other nonentertainment programming and to cover issues of local interest. The latter are to be identified by surveying the community (the "ascertainment" process).[4]

(d) Statutes prohibit broadcast of lotteries; "obscene, indecent or profane" language; fraudulent information; and cigarette advertisements.[5] The latter three rules apply to most electronic transmission media, not just broadcasting.

(e) The Act requires all broadcasters to identify sponsored material. The FCC limits the number of advertisement minutes in each hour of TV and requires TV broadcasters to keep logs of their broadcasts.[6]

These rules were designed for broadcasting. Congress and the FCC have applied some of them to some cable services—a tangled area which will be discussed in Chapter 7. The rules do not apply to common carriers—the one exception is a criminal prohibition on the use of the telephone to make obscene calls.[7] Those who wrote these policies assumed that telephone companies would be carrying others' information, not originating their own.

In addition to federal communications policies, electronic publishers will be governed by state and local laws on obscenity and defamation. These rules usually apply uniformly to all media—including print— although some states and cities are developing new obscenity laws aimed at cable. These laws will be discussed in Chapter 10.

The federal content rules are controversial, especially the political rules and the Fairness Doctrine. The First Amendment bars these kinds of controls on newspapers, and broadcasters feel they should have the same freedom. While many of the content rules represent commonly accepted practice in newspaper publishing, government enforcement of them is unique to broadcasting. Many broadcasters argue that these regulations give government the power to control news, that the threat of complaints to the FCC keeps broadcast news bland and discourages investigative reporting, and that the Equal Time rule reduces campaign coverage by forcing broadcasters to give time to minor candidates if they give it to serious contenders.

Defenders of the content rules reply that broadcasting is not like newspaper publishing because the airwaves belong to the public. A government license is needed to broadcast, and few people can receive one, they argue, so the public is entitled to demand benefits in return for granting licenses. In addition, this side of the argument holds that broadcasting is so powerful that broadcasters should not be allowed to sell time only to candidates they favor or to cover only causes they support.

The Supreme Court has consistently rejected broadcasters' First Amendment challenges to the content rules.[8] The Court has held that the scarcity of broadcast frequencies and the government role in assigning them does make broadcasting different from print publishing and justifies the "public trustee" theory. The First Amendment, says the Court, protects audiences' rights to hear multiple views as well as publishers' rights to say what they want. In other words, as journalists broadcasters may say what they want, but as public trustees they must provide access to others' views. As recently as 1981, the Court reaffirmed the public trustee concept and the "reasonable access" rule, upholding an FCC ruling that CBS should have sold time to the Carter-Mondale committee one year before the 1980 presidential election, overruling CBS' argument that its journalistic judgment should decide when a campaign starts.[9]

In addition, a 1978 Supreme Court decision propounded a second constitutional basis for content regulation—what it called the electronic media's "uniquely pervasive presence in the lives of all Americans." In a case involving "obscene" words spoken over the radio, the Court held that broadcasting may be held to a tighter standard than print "because of the circumstances in which it comes into the home."[10]

These decisions differ sharply from the way the First Amendment applies to print. The Supreme Court has been hostile to any control of print content, protecting publishers against all but the most severe cases of obscenity and defamation. In a classic illustration of the difference in approach, the Court struck down a Florida statute that would have given political candidates a right to reply to newspaper editorials.[11] The Court said "the choice of material to go into a newspaper . . . and treatment of public officials—whether fair or unfair—constitutes the exercise of editorial control and judgment. It has yet to be demonstrated that governmental regulation of this crucial process can be exercised consistent with First Amendment guarantees of a free press. . . ." The judges were not impressed by the argument that in Miami (the city of the newspaper that filed suit) there were two daily newspapers and more than 40 broadcast stations.

While the content rules are constitutional for broadcasting, they have been losing political support recently. One reason is the current antiregulatory mood in Washington—a reaction fed by post-Vietnam and post-Watergate hostility toward government, by a feeling that federal regulation of all kinds has been heavy-handed, and by concern about the cost of regulation at a time of economic insecurity. The other reason is the increase in media outlets. Competition in communications is surging, strengthening the argument that competition will force broadcasters to be fair and to provide what the public wants, without regulatory intervention.

In 1980, these views prompted the FCC to drop the programming and ascertainment rules for radio and to give all broadcasters more flexibility to change formats. In 1981, the FCC asked Congress to repeal the political rules and the Fairness Doctrine. Congress already has lengthened broadcasters' licensee terms and the Senate is considering a deregulation bill. Complete deregulation is unlikely, however, if only because many congressmen feel the Equal Time rule protects them against hostile broadcasters and well-heeled contenders for their jobs.

In addition to the federal regulations, another set of content controls is imposed by state and local obscenity rules and state defamation laws. Both of these kinds of controls are subject to strict First Amendment limits. Obscenity laws must be narrowly drawn and precise in what they ban. For defamation, subjects of legitimate news stories can recover only if they show the publisher acted with malice. Non-federal obscenity rules apply to print publishers; it is not clear whether the federal obscenity laws preempt local action against broadcasters. Defamation laws apply equally to print and broadcasting.

Common carriers, on the other hand, are not covered by content regulations. Their job is to transmit content provided by others, without editing or controlling it, so they are not held responsible except in extraordinary cases. It is not clear where cable fits in this dichotomy, as will be discussed in Chapter 7.

RATE REGULATION

Rate regulation is used to prevent monopolies from overcharging or discriminating among their customers. The classic procedure establishes a return the carrier is entitled to earn on its investment (the "rate base"). The carrier files tariffs that are supposed to cover costs plus generate the authorized return. Regulators evaluate these tariffs to ensure that they allocate costs among customers reasonably and without discrimination. To protect customers from needless additions to the rate base, regulators also rule on carriers' proposals to construct new facilities.

Because of the movement to competition in the telephone industry, FCC common carrier regulation has undergone heavy surgery in the past decade. First, the Commission and the courts dismantled the barriers to entry that excluded competitors. More recently, the Commission has been slicing the rate controls themselves, giving carriers greater freedom to launch new services and to change rates. Transmission rate deregulation has focused on AT&T's competitors, because they do not have any monopoly power. In 1981, however, the FCC took the dramatic step of eliminating rate regulation of equipment and "enhanced" (data processing) services for all carriers—including Bell—on the theory that the competition is strong enough in those areas to obviate the need for regulation.[12] This step is being challenged in court as inconsistent with the Act's common carrier provisions. Congress, however, is working on legislation parallel to the FCC approach.[13] Within a few years, FCC rate regulation is likely to apply only to AT&T's long distance network, much of which will remain a near-monopoly.

Traditional telephone rate regulation continues at the state level, but the maelstrom of competition is about to hit there, too. First, Congress is likely to shift jurisdiction over intrastate toll services from the states to the FCC. This will shrink state authority to local "exchange" services. Second, if the FCC's deregulation decision is upheld by the courts or confirmed by legislation, it will strip the states of jurisdiction over the rates for telephone sets and other equipment. Finally, the states will have to deal with the fact that cable and some over-the-air services will be able to carry voice and data signals in direct competition with local telephone companies. Just as the FCC had to make the shift to competition in the last decade, the states will have to make a similar adjustment in the 1980s.

As for cable, rate regulation has different origins and procedures. The FCC has never regulated cable rates; its rules focus on content and structure. In fact, the FCC preempted local regulation of "pay" cable rates, such as the monthly charges for Home Box Office. However, many cities have written franchises to give them a veto power over the rates cable operators charge subscribers for basic service. Cities do this both to prevent excessive charges—cable is often thought to have monopolistic economic power—and to provide a way to enforce the promises cable operators make in the franchise bidding. This kind of rate regulation is often informal, with no effort to calculate rate bases.

STRUCTURAL REGULATION

In spite of the surge in competition, the number of electronic pipelines to the home remains limited. That bottleneck necessarily limits competition and diversity, and the problem is compounded if one company controls many channels. One may argue that a single owner of multiple channels has an incentive to provide different programming on each and to experiment with some. However, scarcity of channels and concentration of control can give those who own the channels the power to charge excessive rates, discriminate among information providers and impose their views on the public by limiting the information available.

The desires to obtain diversity of viewpoints and competitive pricing were, of course, the key motivations for the original broadcasting content regulations and telephone rate regulations. While those kinds of rules focus on symptoms, structural regulation can deal with the underlying problem—the economic structure of the communications industry. Two decades ago, most of the FCC's structural rules restricted entry and protected monopolies. Today, however, regulation in this area usually is used to increase competition, following the newly accepted theory that competition is the best way to give the public the various services it wants at fair prices. Structural regulation uses four techniques: entry, limits on horizontal integration, mandated access and limits on vertical integration.

Entry Policy

Entry policy works by increasing the number of communications outlets; the FCC has pursued this approach vigorously in the past five years. In broadcasting, the Commission has encouraged the growth of UHF television, has adjusted frequencies to increase the number of radio stations, has authorized low power TV and is likely to authorize satellite-to-home broadcasting. In cable, the FCC has dropped rules that restricted cable growth and opened the skies to the large number of satellites that are now essential to distribute cable programming. In common carriage, the Commission has allowed competitors to set up their own transmission networks and sell their own equipment. These steps have been vital to the new, competitive environment.

Horizontal Limitations

The second kind of structural policy limits the number of channels anyone may control, and current rules limit horizontal integration at both the local and the national levels. In each market, the FCC forbids telephone companies from owning cable television (except in rural areas), restricts joint ownership of newspapers and television stations and forbids ownership of more than one television, one AM and one FM radio station. Some states also bar common ownership in a single market of cable and newspapers. To promote national diversity, FCC rules say that no company may own more than seven television stations, seven AM radio stations and seven FM radio stations. The FCC also says television networks may not become cable operators, although the Commission had made a limited exception for CBS and is reconsidering this overall policy. In addition, FCC Chairman Mark Fowler has said the competition may now be strong enough to obviate the need for many of the existing horizontal restrictions.

Mandated Access

On the other hand, some reformers have long argued that the horizontal rules do not go far enough to ensure that all sides on controversial issues get a chance to be heard, so the government should mandate access to communications channels. The political rules give candidates access rights to broadcast air time, but the government has always refused to mandate any general right of access to the airwaves. The individual TV and radio licensees control who gets on the air and have sole responsibility for broadcasting content. In cable, the FCC originally imposed access requirements for public, educational and government users as well as for commercial groups seeking to lease cable channels. For reasons discussed in Chapter 7, those requirements were struck down by the Supreme Court in 1978, but most of them survive in local franchise arrangements. In the common carrier arena, access has been taken for granted—the essence of common carriage is that the communications facility is available to all.

Vertical Limitations

The last structural tool is restriction of vertical integration. This method is most significant in the telephone area. As the FCC abandons rate regulation, it is turning to structural action to prevent anti-competitive behavior by AT&T. In spite of the new competition, the Bell System dominates the carrier industry. Its intercity network (including short haul links provided by the independent telephone companies) carried 96% of the long distance business in 1981. The Bell local operating companies control local exchange monopolies that cover about 80% of the population. There is general agreement that AT&T's regulated transmission operations should be separated from its unregulated data processing and equipment manufacturing entities. The idea is to prevent Bell from using revenue or monopoly power from the first area to give it an unfair advantage in the second. However, a vigorous debate has raged for four years over the degree and kind of separation needed.

The FCC and Congress chose the device of an arms-length subsidiary for the competitive operations, with the House favoring a greater degree of separation than the Senate. The Justice Department felt that AT&T had to be split up, and in January 1982, it achieved that result. In a settlement of Justice's antitrust suit, AT&T agreed to divest itself of its local exchange operations.

While the new, national AT&T will be much smaller than the old company, it will still combine near monopoly long distance operations with competitive activities. Therefore, the argument about the appropriate separation between these functions will continue. In addition, some observers have expressed similar concerns about other telephone companies (e.g., GTE has both local exchange monopolies and unregulated equipment manufacturing operations) and about vertically integrated cable companies (i.e., companies that both own cable systems and originate programming).

SUMMARY

To sum up the situation, a decade of deregulation has sliced away many of the old federal content and rate regulations and has removed the structural rules that had limited entry. Continued deregulation may further reduce the FCC's role in all three areas. However, there are some contrary trends: the FCC's difficult task of overseeing the transition in the telephone industry, and the new generation of local controls on cable. In any case, all three kinds of rules remain on the books and will affect electronic publishing.

FOOTNOTES

1. 47 U.S.C. 312 (a) (7).
2. The equal time and minimum rate laws are at 47 U.S.C. 315.
3. 47 U.S.C. 315 and 47 C.F.R. 73.1910 and 73.1920.
4. 47 C.F.R. 73.1130; 0.281(a) (8); and 73.4020.
5. 18 U.S.C. 1304 (lotteries); 18 U.S.C. 1464 (obscenity); 18 U.S.C. 1343 (fraud); 15 U.S.C. 1335 (cigarettes).
6. 47 U.S.C. 317; 47 C.F.R. 0.281(a) (7); and 73.1800.
7. 13 U.S.C. 1335.
8. The classic Court decision in this area was *Red Lion Broadcasting, Inc. v. FCC*, 395 U.S. 367 (1969). See also *U.S. v. Associated Press*, 326 U.S. 1

(1945) and *F.C.C. v. National Citizens Committee*, 436 U.S. 775 (1978).
9. *CBS, Inc. v. FCC*, 101 S. Ct. 2813 (1981).
10. *F.C.C. v. Pacifica Foundation*, 438 U.S. 726 (1978).
11. *Miami Herald Publishing Co. v. Tornillo*, 418 U.S. 241 (1974).
12. This decision is called the *Second Computer Inquiry* (Computer II). (FCC Docket No. 20828) It was decided in 1980 and revised on reconsideration in 1981, and it will be before the U.S. Court of Appeals (D.C. Circuit) in 1982.
13. The Senate passed S. 898 in September, 1981. The House Commerce Committee is debating its own common carrier legislation, H.R. 5158.

4

A Communications Policy
for Electronic Publishing

Under current law, the application of content, rate and structural
regulations to electronic publishing depends on the particular transmission medium that a publisher uses. The Communications Act's basic
structure relies on distinctions among over-the-air, telephone and cable
transmissions, even though electronic publishers may send identical
information on all these media. The rules were written in a different era,
when technological distinctions did mark service boundaries, and they
are ripe for change.

Because communications policy is in flux, there is an opportunity to
bend all these regulations into a sensible policy for electronic publishing.
Pristine uniformity is unattainable, but a sensible, reasonably consistent
policy is within reach. This chapter will develop such an approach, and
the next three chapters will spell out how the regulations apply today to
electronic publishing over the three transmission media and will suggest
how to reshape those rules to fit the general policy.

CONTENT REGULATION

When the policy debate on this new medium begins, content regulation
may draw the most attention. Newspapers are likely to become electronic
publishers, and they will push to include this medium under their
constitutional immunity from most content controls. On the other hand,
supporters of content regulation are likely to fight for it, if only to slow the
assault on the rules' coverage of broadcasting. This argument will be
couched, as it has been in broadcasting, as a conflict between the two
goals of the First Amendment—publishers' freedom from censorship and
audiences' right to diversity. The final decisions may well be made in

Congress or the Supreme Court.

In general, content regulation of electronic publishing would do little good and considerable harm. If government intervention is needed to ensure diversity, it should be pursued through structural regulation, without the practical costs and censorship risks of content regulation. However, some content controls are inevitable and a few others may be desirable.

Lack of Scarcity

There are several reasons to avoid content controls. First, the constitutional basis for the broadcast content rules is scarcity, and electronic publishing offers the potential for abundance. Narrowband teletext may be even more competitive than radio—it can be provided on each TV and MDS station, each FM radio station and each cable channel. (As will be discussed in Chapter 5, FCC regulations currently limit some of these options, but those rules can and should be changed.) Broadband teletext has fewer outlets, but cable and MDS provide at least the potential for a choice, and low power TV and DBS may provide more options in a few years. As for videotext, the technology makes possible an unlimited number of data bases, each with an unlimited number of pages. While economics may limit the number of local videotext gateways, additional entry always will be possible, and subscribers most likely will be able to go directly or through gateways to reach a vast number of data bases around the country.

If electronic publishing proves commercially attractive and if appropriate structural policies are adopted, this should be an extremely competitive business. Instead of the lowest-common-denominator programming the television networks often provide, electronic publishers will have an economic incentive to serve the special interests of any substantial audience. Vigorous competition will push electronic publishers to provide whatever the public wants, and content rules are more likely to hinder than help that effort.

Advocates of regulation may reply that public demand for electronic publishing will be insufficient to support all the competition that technology makes possible or that some submarkets—such as broadband teletext—may not be competitive. The answer to this position is that if the public is not using the service, then there is little need to regulate it. As for market definition, it depends on the degree to which consumers view products as interchangeable, and such consumer attitudes for electronic publishing are not yet known. Broadband teletext may be a discrete market, but it is also possible that all of teletext will turn out to be directly competitive with newspapers. Speculation is a poor basis for regulation.

In any case, the Supreme Court has considered and rejected the argument that content regulation may be imposed on publishers because economics limits their number.[1] This was the key holding in the decision mentioned in Chapter 3 that overruled Florida's reply law for newspapers. Technological scarcity—the need for federal licensing to allocate use of a scarce public resource—is the prime constitutional justification for broadcasting content regulation, and it is a weak basis to extend such regulation to electronic publishing.

Defenders of the content rules also contend that no matter how many channels are available, well-funded proponents of establishment views are bound to dominate the public dialogue, and some requirement of balance is needed to give poorly funded and unconventional arguments a chance to be heard. This concern stems from the inequitable distribution of resources in our society, not any particular communication technology, and it must be weighed against the difficulty and danger of government decisions on which the information the public "needs" or on how to "balance" views. In the absence of scarcity, the First Amendment seems to bar regulation, but constitutional principles in this area remain cloudy.

Access by Choice

The second reason to eschew content control is that electronic publishing is fundamentally different from broadcasting in the way it reaches people. Broadcasting gives its audience limited control over or advance notice of the content to be disseminated. For example, in the Supreme Court case, detailed in Chapter 10, that said this "pervasive" character justifies regulation, a child heard some indecent words on the car radio before his father could turn it off.[2] In electronic publishing, by contrast, the user must take an action—by pushing buttons—to look at a page of information. Users can decide which pages to display and which to ignore. This medium will not "pervade" our homes.

Of course, children may skim through electronic publishing pages and stumble on offensive material, but the same is true of print. Some obscenity laws are certain to apply, as will be discussed later. But the user's relationship to electronic publishing is more like print than broadcasting, and the need and constitutional support for content regulation are correspondingly weaker.

Overburden of Regulation

Third, the content rules would impose substantial burdens and could even kill some useful services. For example, broadband teletext can provide about 5000 pages per channel, and videotext can handle many more. Many of these pages would be updated daily or hourly and would come from information providers not now covered by FCC regulations, such as newspapers and magazine publishers. Some of these information providers would send their pages electronically for automatic injection into the system's computer, without any involvement by the system operator.

Complaints about "fairness" and "balance" in this mass of information would be inevitable. System operators could be fined or even lose FCC licenses for content that violates the rules. Operators subject to the content rules therefore would be required to review every page—a heavy overhead cost for a fledgling service. Of course, print publishers must check content; apart from professional responsibility they can be liable for obscenity and defamation. The difference is that the Communications Act imposes additional requirements unfamiliar to many print publishers, and it places full responsibility for content on the system operator. There is no way to make the information provider assume the liability. Moreover, information providers, such as newspapers, that are unfamiliar with the FCC content rules or find them objectionable on principle might be reluctant to contribute to electronic data bases in the first place.

Of course, content review for a 200-page VBI teletext service would be easy to do, but "access" or "balance" requirements could create problems for narrowband teletext. These systems seem likely to gain user acceptance by maintaining a permanent structure, so that the traffic report, for example, always appears on the same numbered page. The data base is so small that any regulation that forces the operator to add pages could disrupt this structure. For example, a television station might want to devote its 200 pages to continuously updated stock or commodity prices. Such a service could be useful to businessmen or farmers, and the system could provide it inexpensively by automatically feeding the pages from a wire service, with minimal capital or personnel costs. Such an operation would be impossible, however, if the data base were required to incude pages on controversial issues, local interests or political candidates.

The FCC's restrictions on advertising also can be troublesome because commercials on electronic publishing will work differently than those on regular television. Information pages may be dedicated to advertising (e.g., an airline schedule or an announcement of a sale) or may be sponsored (e.g., a news page may carry a sponsor's logo). Some data bases may consist entirely of such pages. Because this may be the only practical basis for "free" electronic publishing services, the restrictions on the number of advertisements per hour that now apply to television are wholly inappropriate for this new medium.

"Balance" Requirement Complications

Fourth, enforcement of the content rules would create unusual constitutional and practical problems for electronic publishing . Application of a "balance" requirement to a massive data base that is full of expressions of opinion taken from multiple sources presents even more danger of government interference with editorial discretion —as well as practical difficulty—than it does for normal broadcasting. Moreover, the rules may be counterproductive. To avoid regulatory problems, electronic publishers covered by content controls may exclude opinions and controversial material altogether. This is already happening in at least one case: editorials are not being used in the teletext experiment on Los Angeles public broadcasting station KCET due to fear of triggering costly Fairness Doctrine obligations.

Discouragement of Services

Fifth, application of the content rules could preclude some desirable services. For example, a broadcaster or cable operator might want to operate a broadband teletext or a videotext service as a carrier or a gateway, providing transmission and perhaps data processing to anyone who wants to insert pages without controlling content at all. Such an arrangement would be comparable to electronic publishing over telephone lines, in which the information provider is responsible for the content and the carrier has neither control nor responsibility.

This kind of operation is desirable because it would promote diversity. In particular, it would provide a forum for small information providers who cannot afford to buy their own computers but want to be able to communicate directly to the public, without adhering to a large publisher's format or content rules. The problem is that the system operators that are covered by the FCC's content rules retain full responsibility for content, no matter who creates it. Such liability would force them to control content and preclude true carrier or gateway services.

Restricting Competition

The final argument against the content rules is that it would be unfair and anticompetitive to apply them to some electronic publishing services and not others. For all the reasons cited above, compliance with content rules can cost money and limit services. Under present law and regulations, the key federal content rules do not apply to some over-the-air signals, to cable channels that are not controlled by the cable company, or to telephone lines. Whatever the merits, there is little likelihood in the current political climate that the rules will be extended to these media. The immune media, therefore, would have a significant competitive advantage. This is particularly troubling because narrowband broadcast teletext already suffers the handicap of limited capacity. The additional burden of content regulation could discourage some broadcasters from entering the business at all.

Intense competition faced by new communications technologies has two effects: 1) it forces the provider to tailor his service to public demand and therefore reduces the need for regulation, and 2) it reduces the size of the audience and thereby increases the burden of regulation. In the case of electronic publishing, competition should be given the chance to shape content, without government intervention.

Needed Regulations

This policy does not mean complete immunity from content liability. As detailed in Chapter 10, content regulation is inevitable for obscenity and defamation. In those areas, the best approach is to treat electronic publishers the same as print publishers. However, system operators that take all their content from others and exercise no editorial contract should be viewed as carriers and exempted from liability.

In addition, at least two of the Communications Act's individual rules are not touched by most of the arguments against regulation and would have significant advantages if applied to electronic publishing. One is the law that requires broadcasters to identify sponsored material. Such a rule could be satisfied on an electronic page by inserting the heading, "advertisement"; responsible newspapers use that approach for ads that are written to resemble news stories. If oil companies supply teletext pages on energy policy, for example, the pages should indicate this. Such a requirement would help the public and impose little burden on the service.

The other law is the part of the Equal Time rule that deals with political advertising. This regulation prevents broadcasters from selling time to a favored candidate and refusing it to others. If electronic publishing becomes a mass medium, candidates should have the same protection, so they can buy pages on equal terms. Unlike the Fairness Doctrine, this policy is objective; it does not require regulators to second guess editorial judgments. In addition, this rule need not pose practical problems. Videotext and broadband teletext will have plenty of capacity to handle political advertisements. Narrowband teletext may not have such

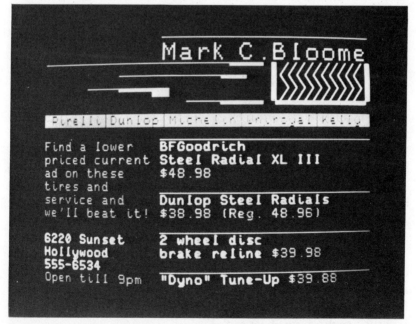

Typical advertisement appearing on the Antiope videotext system. Most frames, such as this one, do not carry a heading to identify them as advertisements. Courtesy Antiope.

capacity; in such cases the Act allows the FCC to let the operator refuse all political ads, as Chapter 5 explains.

In reality, there is little chance that these two rules will be applied to the whole range of electronic publishing transmission media. Whatever Congress and the Supreme Court make of the scarcity rationale for broadcast teletext, they are hardly likely to find it applies to telephone-based videotext. Courts work from analogies, and the closest existing model to videotext is print publishing. Print is not completely immune from regulation, but the Florida decision discussed earlier indicates the Court would be reluctant to let Congress apply the sponsorship or Equal Time rules to newspapers.

Lack of uniformity for these two policies would not be a significant handicap on those who are covered. Therefore, the pragmatic answer is to keep the two rules for broadcast teletext and let a few years of practical experience determine whether they should be extended to the other media or dropped.

In conclusion, content regulation of electronic publishing generally should follow the print model of minimum intervention. Many electronic publishers will act voluntarily to provide balance and fairness, as do their responsible print brethren. Others will be careless and unscrupulous, as are some print publishers. In the print media our society has chosen to live with those problems rather than take the risks of censorship. We should take the same road in electronics.

RATE REGULATION

Rate regulation can affect electronic publishing either by controlling the charges for transmission or by directly controlling the rates for information services. The first category currently covers use of telephone lines, and rate controls may be applied to cable systems if they operate as carriers. This kind of regulation applies to transmission for any purpose, not just electronic publishing. While the policy issues are beyond the scope of this book, trends in telephone transmission rates will affect the development of videotext; they will be discussed in Chapter 6.

Direct rate regulation of electronic publishing could cover the charges customers pay to receive the information or the fees advertisers and other information providers pay to put pages into the data base. Neither variety is being imposed or is in prospect, but it is useful to outline the reasons that such controls are undesirable.

In general, the purpose of rate regulation is to protect consumers against a monopolist's power to overprice or discriminate. In this area, if sensible structural rules are set, there should be no monopolies in electronic publishing. Moreover, information rate regulation could do several kinds of damage.

First, such controls could scare off potential service providers. Many entrepreneurs would judge that regulation would keep profits lower than in similarly speculative investments in unregulated industries.

Second, rate regulation makes businesses inflexible. It imposes a delay (often called "regulatory lag") between the time tariffs are filed proposing service and rate changes and the time they go into effect. This delay would make it hard for electronic publishers to respond to market demands and compete with unregulated information providers, such as newspapers.

Third, rate regulation distorts incentives. Instead of responding to marketplace forces, system operators would have incentives to inflate their rate bases—increasing their dollar return—by building more equipment than they need. Rate regulation also would pull money and management time from operations to regulatory proceedings.

Fourth, traditional rate regulation might force regulators to review operators' decisions on the value of individual pieces of information or decide how to apportion the investment in a computer used for electronic publishing and other services. Such decisions would be difficult to make.

Finally, rate regulation poses the threat of government control over information content. Electronic publishers might skew coverage of public affairs to please those who control their profits.

For all these reasons, traditional rate regulation could do serious harm to novel services struggling to find their niche in a risky and competitive marketplace. If competition does flourish, it should keep rates reasonable without any of these costs.

STRUCTURAL REGULATION

The proposed approach of minimal regulation for content and rates hinges on electronic publishing's potential to be competitive, and competition depends on the availability and ownership of electronic pipelines to the home. Structural action to ensure diversity and competition, therefore, is the one area where regulation may be needed.

Open Entry and Horizontal Integration

Open entry is a vital ingredient of the needed structural policy. The FCC took dramatic steps in the past decade to increase the number of electronic pipelines to the home, and this movement should continue. As Chapter 5 explains, the Commission should lift the rules that limit the kinds of teletext services broadcasters can offer, such as rules that limit the FM subcarrier to subscription services. The FCC also should move promptly to establish low power TV and DBS. In addition, new over-the-air technologies, such as "cellular radio," offer the potential for competition with the local telephone exchange. The FCC should encourage such competition.

The second structural policy area is horizontal integration. It is important to ensure diverse ownership of communications outlets in each market, and the existing media ownership rules are intended to do this job. The advent of electronic publishing does not appear to require any new horizontal rules or suggest elimination of any old ones.

Access and vertical integration pose the most important structural issues for electronic publishing. There is a limited number of channels to the home, and economics may also limit the number of videotext gateways in each market. Many of the companies that control transmission channels are also becoming data base managers and information providers, and tend to see others in those businesses as competitors; they may want to keep them off their channels and out of their gateways. The result is a threat to diversity and competition.

Separations and Access Rules

One response is a "separations" policy. Under this approach, the transmission company is limited to carriage and may not provide any information content over its own lines. Britain uses this policy for videotext; the British Post Office provides transmission but takes all its information pages from independent information providers.

The problem with separations is that if transmission is divorced from content, some services may be sacrificed. Unlike most other countries experimenting with electronic publishing, the United States has neither government subsidies nor a monopoly system operator similar to a European Post, Telephone and Telegraph Ministry. The private companies that provide transmission—notably broadcasters and cable companies—have been the leaders in developing teletext and videotext in the United States, and they seem the most likely to continue making the risky investments that are needed. If these companies are cut out of providing content, they may lose the incentive to play in the game.

"Access" is the other alternative: let the transmission company provide content but require it to give others access to the channel. Unfortunately, the transmission company has an incentive to treat its content better than its competitors', and it is difficult to draw the line between discrimination and reasonable business judgments. Policing equal treatment is a regulatory swamp, particularly if there are more would-be information providers than space in the transmission medium. The transmission company would have to decide who gets on the system, how much they pay, what kind of service they get and so on. The potential for favoritism in such decisions is infinite, as is the potential for paperwork and delay if regulators have to evaluate all the complaints.

To increase transmission companies' incentives to invest, a separations policy could allow the transmission company to provide the gateway and data base management functions. Thus, in Britain the Post Office manages the data base and bills the customers. The separations rule is imposed at the point where the information enters computer. However, this approach is impractical for access. It is difficult enough to determine whether a company is giving its competitors the same transmission services as it gives itself; it is almost impossible to make such judgments about a data base. Organizing a data base demands thousands of arbitrary indexing decisions; subjecting all those decisions to regulatory challenge would be a bureaucratic nightmare.

The need for separations or access rules depends on the vigor of competition—the number of channels and gateways available to information providers. In narrowband teletext, the problem is remote. This service can use many potential conduits to the home, and FCC entry policies are creating more.

Videotext, by contrast, depends on local telephone exchanges, and those exchanges are still monopolies. The telephone network always has been open to access by all, but now that some telephone companies are also becoming information providers, there are difficult issues to deal with. A debate is raging over imposing separations; this will be discussed in Chapter 6.

Cable complicates this dichotomy for two reasons: 1) the broadband teletext it can provide is so much more powerful than narrowband that it might be considered a separate market; and 2) cable eventually will provide an alternative medium for videotext. Cable has such economic power that structural intervention may be desirable, as discussed in Chapter 7.

By the end of the decade, the market structure may be further changed if telephone companies install optical fiber, which can provide at least as much capacity as cable, or if two-way radio becomes another videotext distribution system. For these reasons, any separations or access rules that are imposed should be kept flexible, so that they can be revised as economic structures become clearer and shift with technology.

To sum up: a communications policy for electronic publishing should rely on competition rather than content or rate regulation. Structural action—to promote entry and require separation or access—is the best way to ensure competition. The next three chapters will apply those principles to the rules that govern the three transmission media.

FOOTNOTES

1. *Miami Herald Publishing Co. v. Tornillo,* 418 U.S. 241 (1974).
2. *F.C.C. v. Pacifica Foundation,* 438 U.S. 726 (1978).

5

Over-The-Air Teletext

The FCC controls use of the ratio spectrum by allocating bands of frequencies to particular services, such as radio and television. The Commission classifies each service under a broad category: in addition to the categories in the Communications Act—broadcasting, common carriage and nonbroadcast private radio—the FCC has occasionally improvised "hybrid" categories. The category determines the general outline for the rules governing the service, and the FCC writes individual regulations to fill in the specifics.

For teletext on MDS, the regulatory status is already established. When the FCC invented MDS it had data services in mind, so its rules allow teletext operations today. The Commission classified MDS as common carriage rather than broadcasting, so the content rules do not apply.[1] The regulations do limit MDS to subscription services, in part to distinguish it from "broadcasting,"and this restriction is likely to remain because MDS uses frequencies that can be received only with a special antenna that must be wired to the television set.

Because the MDS licensee is a carrier, it cannot originate content. Instead, the licensee operates the transmitter and leases the channel to a content provider. For teletext, the MDS licensee either may turn over the whole channel to an electronic publisher or may lease the regular signal for pay TV and lease the VBI to a separate teletext provider. MDS is subject to rate regulation, but the regulators routinely approve whatever rates licensees charge.

If teletext on MDS is simple, teletext on TV and radio channels raises some tricky problems. These are broadcast services, but the FCC is using the "hybrid" rubric for narrowband teletext. The Commission adopted hybrid classification for all services on the FM subcarrier years ago, and the agency proposed similar status for VBI teletext in late 1981. However, this approach rests on shaky legal ground, and the Commission has said nothing about broadband broadcast teletext. It is therefore important to evaluate each of the possible classifications.

COMMON CARRIAGE

In theory, the FCC might treat teletext on radio and TV as common carriage. Such a policy would have some advantages: it would avoid content regulation and establish parallel treatment with MDS and telephone-based services, and it could be administered to provide access rights for numbers of information providers. However, common carrier classification would face overwhelming legal and practical obstacles.

On the legal side, the Communications Act probably kills this option by saying that "a person engaged in radio broadcasting shall not . . . be deemed a common carrier."[2] The FCC might try to evade this provision for VBI teletext and the FM subcarrier by reallocating the relevant portions of these signals out of the TV and radio services. However, these transmissions are integral parts of the larger signals—one cannot exist without the other. If the FCC treated them as common carriage, it would be forcing broadcasters to carry someone else's content on their channels. That probably would violate the Act.

From a practical perspective, VBI lines and the FM subcarrier can be used for purposes other than teletext. Reallocation could foreclose such uses before anyone knows how viable broadcast teletext will be or how desirable the alternatives may be. The access that could be required under common carriage would achieve little for a data base of a few hundred pages and could make the service less attractive to the public. If access were required, broadcasters, already concerned that teletext will compete with regular television, would resist providing teletext at all. Since the broadcaster controls the transmitter that creates the signal, the FCC would find it hard to force broadcasters to turn over a portion of that signal to others and almost impossible to enforce requirements on signal quality.

For all these reasons, the FCC seems certain to let TV and radio licensees continue to control the entire signal, limiting the options to "hybrid" and broadcast treatment.

"HYBRID" CLASSIFICATION

The Communications Act makes no provision for "hybrids," but it does give the Commission broad discretion to experiment with new uses of the spectrum.[3] The Commission used that authority 20 years ago to develop a special classification for the FM subcarrier—the Subsidiary Communication Authorization (SCA). The SCA is a license to transmit an extra signal to subscribers in addition to the regular radio programming. Originally, the SCA was used for transmission of uninterrupted background music to special decoders in offices, shops and so on, so content issues never came up. Several years ago, however, the rules were broadened to cover many SCA uses, including teletext.[4]

The FCC imposes no rate regulation on SCAs; nor does it enforce the political rules and the Fairness Doctrine here. The SCA rules require only that the service be "of a broadcast nature" and be provided on a subscription basis. The broadcaster may lease the SCA to another content provider but must retain control over the material transmitted.

The FCC has proposed to take a similar approach to VBI teletext. In draft rules issued for public comment in November 1981, the Commission said it planned to treat this service as "ancillary" to broadcasting. Its announcement stated that broadcasters could provide teletext on a subscription or advertiser-supported basis and would not be subject to "performance standards"—meaning that no content rules will apply.

Legal Precedent

The problem with this regulation-free approach is that it rests on shaky legal foundations. The only precedent for the VBI decision is the SCA rule, and that was never challenged. The Commission's decision not to apply the Fairness Doctrine or political broadcast rules to SCAs was in response to a query from a service intended for the blind, that airs volunteers reading newspapers aloud.[5] Great battles over content seemed unlikely. Even in that case, the FCC said that if actual operations raise Fairness Doctrine problems, the FCC will "promptly review the whole matter." The decision is silent on other content rules, such as those affecting advertising and obscenity. When it made this decision, the Commission was hardly thinking about a service that might create its own content for mass audiences.

The legality of the "hybrid" approach could be attacked in two ways:

1) the FM subcarrier and the VBI lines are part of the regular broadcast signals and should not be treated as something different, and 2) teletext falls under the statutory definition of "broadcasting."

The first argument can be refuted easily. The Act places no restriction on the Commission's discretion to allocate spectrum—there is no requirement that all parts of a channel be treated identically. The SCA is a good example of this approach: the split of an FM frequency into a broadcast service and a hybrid service has stood unchallenged for two decades. Similarly, the FCC allows some television stations to operate as regular, free broadcasters during some hours and switch to subscription service—under different rules—during other hours.

Definition of "Broadcasting"

However, the second issue presents serious problems. To classify teletext as a "hybrid" and free it from content regulations, the FCC must find that it does not fall under the statutory definition of "broadcasting": "the dissemination of radio communications intended to be received by the public, directly or by the intermediary of relay stations."[6] On their face, these words certainly seem to cover teletext.

There are two possible arguments to get around this barrier: 1) Congress did not mean to cover electronic publishing when it used the word "broadcasting," and 2) some teletext services are not intended for the public at large.

The differences between teletext and broadcasting were outlined in Chapter 4. To recap, teletext carries data, rather than TV programs. The user controls the information received by selecting particular pages for display. Teletext looks and is used more like print publishing than television. Thus, while broadcast teletext certainly is "dissemination of radio signals," the Commission may argue it is not "broadcasting."

There is some precedent for this kind of creative semantics, such as the FCC's novel regulatory scheme for cable television. Cable somewhat resembles broadcasting and somewhat resembles common carriage, but the courts upheld the FCC when it decided that cable belonged in neither pigeonhole and needed its own special rules.

On the other hand, it is hard to be moved by arguments about what Congress "meant" in 1934, when few legislators had ever heard of television, much less teletext. What Congress clearly did intend was to regulate a powerful new mass medium that uses the airwaves. Content rules such as the Equal Time and Fairness Doctrine were adopted to govern the way information is disseminated to the public over the air. While judges can find ways to uphold the "hybrid" approach, the Act's literal words and apparent intent argue for treating teletext as broadcasting.

The second argument only applies to subscription services. The theory here is that because such services are intended only for limited groups, they are not for "the public" and hence are not "broadcasting." The FCC based its SCA classification on this distinction, asserting that rules such as the Fairness Doctrine do not apply because the service is not "broadcasting."

This approach is now generally accepted in the context of signal piracy. A section of the Communications Act bars unauthorized interception of signals except those which are "for the use of the general public."[7] Under this statute, operators of subscription services have sued sellers and manufacturers of equipment that allows people to intercept signals without paying for them. The defendants have argued that such signals are "broadcasting" and available to all. In the case of the SCA, the broadcasters won this fight in court 15 years ago.[8] In the past year, subscription television operators also have won key decisions holding that their signals are not "broadcasting" because they are intended for limited groups.[9]

These decisions support classifying subscriber teletext as a "hybrid," but they are not conclusive. As a U.S. Court of Appeals pointed out in the most recent pay television piracy case, "broadcasting" may have one meaning for the interception provision and another for the content rules.[10] Court review of this issue would focus on Congress' intentions, and the piracy provision certainly has a different purpose than for content rules. A court might well decide that if subscription teletext provides information to large numbers of people, it is the kind of service covered under the Act's content provisions.

Moreover, there are practical problems with a theory that allows "hybrid" classification only for subscription teletext. This arrangement would push television stations to provide "pay" instead of "free" services. If licensees were required to file and seek permission before changing from one category to the other, experiments might be discouraged and operators might lock into "pay" services for fear of losing the opportunity of returning to them. The FCC's proposed teletext rules avoid this problem by allowing broadcasters to provide either service. That is good policy, but it means the "piracy" precedent will not help.

In sum, there is major doubt whether the FCC's approach will hold up. The answer will await several years of litigation, and the final decision is likely to depend on the particular case. For example, if a broadcaster puts one candidate's position paper into his data base but refuses to do so for the opponent, a court would most likely decide that the Equal Time law applies no matter what the FCC has determined.

Even if the "hybrid" approach does prevail, some content rules will remain. The statutory ban on cigarette advertising applies to all electronic media subject to FCC jurisdiction.[11] The ban on "obscene, indecent and profane material" applies to any "means of radio communication" and therefore will cover VBI teletext no matter how it is classified.[12] The ban on lottery information covers all radio stations and probably applies to "hybrid" teletext.[13] Legislation would be needed to treat these areas the way they are treated for print media.

Definitional Problems

One long-term problem with the "hybrid" approach that the FCC seems to have ignored is the difficulty of defining the service. The definition in the proposed rules limits teletext to transmission of data for visual display; that rightfully has been criticized as preventing use of the VBI to download computer software. The Commission can and should allow broadcasters to use their VBIs for any kind of service. On the other hand, any definition that puts teletext in a different regulatory category than television is bound to run into trouble. The technical difference is that teletext is digitalized and television is analog, but engineers are developing systems that will transmit digitally coded photographs. If that does not cross the line into television, what about animation? Eventually, services that look identical to the viewer may be treated differently and courts will be hard pressed to sustain such arbitrary arrangements.

Regular television also is expanding toward teletext. For example, the "Nite-Owl" program now running on a Chicago TV station is a text-only service that uses a full TV channel. This service requires no decoder and each page is broadcast for a few seconds. Otherwise, it resembles teletext, but the proposed rules would leave it classified as broadcasting because it uses a full channel.

If teletext succeeds, more broadcasters are bound to seek the tenfold increase in page capacity that full-channel teletext offers. If the FCC says

```
MECCA BOOKMAKERS      2070a           0p
   RACING RESULTS-RACING RESULTS

Results for MONDAY 22-3-82

Key          1st Race Weather  Going

1 BRISTOL........1-33  FINE    GOOD
2 WOLVERHAMPTON..2-00  FINE    G-SFT
3 PLUMPTON.......2-15  FINE    SOFT
4 CARLISLE.......2-15  FINE    SOFT

Results for SATURDAY 20-3-82

5 LINGFIELD
6 NEWCASTLE
7 UTTOXETER

      Key # for Todays Tricast Races
             Key 0 Main Page
```

Electronic page from the Prestel videotext system displaying racing results. Although broadcasting such information is legal, some may argue that it encourages gambling. Courtesy Prestel.

that full-channel service is covered by different rules than VBI teletext, then it will have completely different rules for identical services, distinguished only on the basis of how much bandwidth they occupy. But if the FCC says that full-channel teletext also is "hybrid" rather than broadcasting, it will be on extremely weak legal ground. The only way to get certainty and consistency under the "hybrid" label is with legislation.

BROADCAST REGULATION

If the courts or the FCC decide that broadcast teletext is "broadcasting," the Commission still will have leeway to minimize regulation. The FCC can exempt teletext of all kinds from its own content rules, and it can look to the regular radio and televison services to satisfy some of the statutory requirements for SCA and VBI operations.

Flexibility

The Commission clearly has the power to retract its own rules. In 1980 the FCC designed minimal regulatory programs for two other broadcast services that offer good precedents for teletext. The new "low power" television service is "broadcasting," but the FCC drafted special rules to give licensees great flexibility on program origination, ownership and technical requirements. Similarly, the FCC's radio deregulation decision relieved radio licensees of the requirements to provide certain kinds of community programming, limit advertising minutes and maintain program logs.

For VBI teletext, the Commission's proposed rules are terse, but they do seem to give operators complete flexibility. Broadcasters would have no obligation to include pages on local matters. They would be free to contract out for all the data base content, although they would remain legally responsible for it. There would be no limits on the number of advertisements in the data base. Broadcasters would be able to operate on a "pay" or "free" basis and to switch freely from one status to the other.

One complication of treating teletext as broadcasting involves the use of "addressed" messages. One possible use of the technology is for "electronic mail"—messages sent to small groups or individuals, with each person's decoder programmed to receive only the intended messages. The FCC's proposed teletext rules allow subscription services and say nothing about the number of subscribers, so addressed services seem permissible. The uncertainty would be greater if teletext were classified as "broadcasting," because that term connotes a substantial audience. Nevertheless, the courts are likely to sympathize with the Commission's desire to provide total flexibility. The law is not explicit, so an FCC decision allowing addressed teletext probably would be upheld no matter which category is chosen.

Fairness and Equal Time Rules

As for the statutory content rules, if the "hybrid" approach fails the Commission can write new rules that treat teletext as an individual television program, rather than a separate service. Under this arrangement, the licensee's regular radio or TV programming would satisfy the Fairness Doctrine obligation to cover controversial issues of public importance.

The approach would be similar for the other part of the Doctrine—the requirement that coverage be balanced—although that area is trickier. For example, a station might use a newspaper column attacking abortion as a teletext page, and a pro-abortion group might file a Fairness complaint demanding that it be given a page to present their side. In such a case, the FCC probably would rule that the station has no such obligation as long as it covered the issue fairly in its overall teletext and television programming. Some might argue that teletext and television will have different audiences, so balance should be handled separately, but the statute does not require such meticulous balancing any more than it requires individual news programs to present both sides.

Similarly, the Commission could rule that a narrowband data base is so small that a licensee reasonably could refuse to let political candidates buy pages. The FCC would have more difficulty making such a finding for a full channel service, but a right for political candidates to buy pages in a 5000-page magazine should do little harm and might be good for public understanding of campaign issues.

The most important content rule that would still apply under the broadcasting rubric is Equal Time. If this law applies and if one political candidate were given or sold a teletext page, the licensee would be required to give an "equal opportunity" to other candidates for that office.

As discussed in Chapter 4, when applied to paid advertising this requirement would do no harm and would have the benefit of preventing system operators from selling time to favored candidates and excluding others. As it applies to "free" time, however, the Equal Time rule would be damaging. Once large numbers of people have teletext decoders, this technology may prove a useful way for stations to inform the electorate about political candidates. Stations might offer each major candidate a few teletext pages to summarize their backgrounds and positions. Voters would be able to call up this information when they want it, instead of picking it up haphazardly from campaign ads and news stories. However, the Equal Time rule would force the station to include such pages for all candidates, including those from minor parties. In many elections so many minor candidates run that such a requirement would destroy the entire concept.

Of course, broadcasters have long expressed the same criticism of Equal Time—that it prevents them from staging debates and arranging special programs and thereby reduces the quality of campaign coverage. Since the issues are the same, there is no argument for special treatment for teletext on this matter.

Finally, as mentioned earlier, the statutory bans on obscene, indecent and profane material, lottery information and cigarette ads apply whether teletext is considered "hybrid" or broadcasting.

CONCLUSION

In sum, the broadcasting approach permits a quite reasonable set of rules for VBI and FM subcarrier teletext. The complications will come if broadcasters want to turn entire TV channels over to teletext. In that case, there would be no regular TV programming to satisfy the content rules, so all the statutory rules would apply. The Commission also might have trouble deciding whether to allow such a service on channels dedicated to television—especially after pronouncing that teletext is different from television and should not be considered broadcasting at all. Legal gymnastics at the FCC would make full-channel over-the-air electronic publishing possible, but only legislation could sort out the resulting legal tangle.

FOOTNOTES

1. 47 C.F.R. 21.900-21.908.
2. 47 U.S.C. § 153(h).
3. 47 U.S.C. § 303
4. 47 C.F.R. § 73.293-295.
5. *Greater Washington Educ. Telecommunications Assn.*, 49 F.C.C.2d 948 (1974).
6. 47 U.S.C. § 153(o).
7. 47 U.S.C. § 605.
8. *KMLA Broadcasting Corp. v. Twentieth Century Cigarette Vendor Corp.*, 264 F. Supp . 35 (C.D. Cal. 1967).
9. *Chartwell Communications Group v. Westbrook*, 637 F.2d 459 (6th Cir., 1980); *National Subscription Television v. Salt TV*, 644 F.2d 820 (9th Cir., 1981).
10. *National Subscription, supra.*
11. 15 U.S.C. 1335.
12. 47 U.S.C. 317.
13. 18 U.S.C. 1304.

6

Telephone Videotext

The telephone network is the most powerful transmission medium for electronic publishing. It reaches almost everyone, and because it is two-way it can link subscribers to an unlimited number of data bases. The telephone does have limitations: its copper wires move data relatively slowly, and many local networks have insufficient capacity to handle simultaneous, prolonged videotext operations by large numbers of people. However, the telephone companies are currently working to increase the capabilities of the existing network, and they may eventually install high-capacity optical fiber in place of wires.

The issues discussed here involving the telephone network apply only to videotext. Telephone lines are not likely to carry teletext because this service requires continuous transmission of many pages down all the lines—it would swamp the network.

In the area of content regulation, there are two federal laws affecting telephone-delivered videotext: a criminal prohibition on use of the telephone to make "any comment, request, suggestion or proposal which is lewd, lascivious, filthy or indecent"[1] and a ban on cigarette advertising.[2] The first provision is intended for obscene telephone calls. It could cover use of videotext to advertise X-rated movies or for personal classifieds, but federal prosecutors are likely to leave such cases to local authorities. As a practical matter, content issues for this technology will be handled at the state and local levels, as discussed in Chapter 10.

Economic and structural regulation, however, already is the subject of great controversy. The problem is that telephone videotext is a competitive service that depends on a monopoly network. The questions whether carriers should themselves become electronic publishers, how to regulate them if they do and how to provide access to their networks by others are key issues in the legislation to rewrite common carrier law, now pending in Congress.

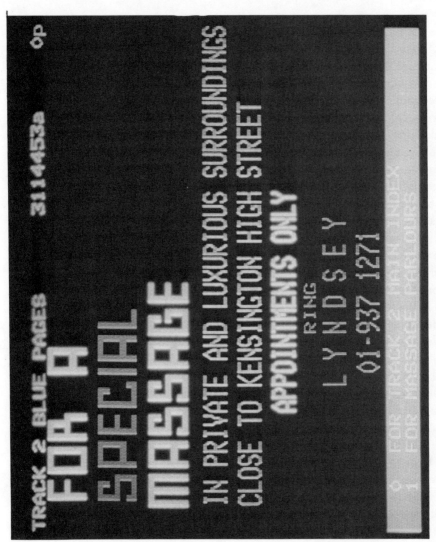

Prestel frame displaying what may be considered questionable material. The issue of content regulation may be raised here. Courtesy Prestel.

BACKGROUND: COMPUTER II
AND THE ANTITRUST SETTLEMENT

Until 1980, the Federal Communications Commission defined its jurisdiction to cover telecommunications but not data processing. At the borderline, predominantly communications services—"hybrid communications"—were regulated; "hybrid data processing" was not.

The FCC did not have occasion to classify videotext under this scheme. If it had done so, it probably would have opted for hybrid data processing, but it might well have treated services related directly to the telephone system, such as electronic directory assistance, as hybrid communications.

These old rules let telephone companies provide hybrid data processing through separate subsidiaries. However, AT&T was covered by a 1956 antitrust consent decree that restricted it to services "subject to" regulation. Therefore, everyone assumed that AT&T was excluded from hybrid data processing, including most videotext services.

This arrangement had two problems. First, the merger of computer and communications technology made line drawing increasingly difficult. Videotext is one example: it is both communications and data processing. Second, AT&T was eager to enter the dynamic computer/communications market, and many sympathizers thought its entry would bring increased and improved services.

Computer II

In 1980 the Commission revamped the old rules with its *Computer II* decision.[3] Its new framework has two categories of services: "basic" and "enhanced."

"Basic service" is the "common carrier offering of transmission capacity for the movement of information." A basic service may use computers for transmission, but it does not manipulate the information content. It is regulated under the Communications Act's common carriage rules.

"Enhanced service" covers any offering over a telecommunications network which is more than basic transmission, including data storage and retrieval. This category is not regulated now, although the

Commission's decision said it might impose regulation in the future if competition in any market proves inadequate. Thus, videotext is to be unregulated under *Computer II,* as the Commission noted in its decision. Terminals and other equipment associated with videotext also are unregulated.

The Commission adopted this policy because it wanted to limit economic regulation to basic services. The FCC felt that there was a competitive marketplace for enhanced services, as well as for telecommunications equipment, so regulation was not needed and would actually impede technological advances and response to consumer demands. In addition, the Commission wanted to remove the legal uncertainties about AT&T offerings of enhanced services. Because such services remain "subject to" regulation, the FCC calculated that its decision would let Bell provide them on an unregulated basis without running afoul of the consent decree.

The danger of this policy was that AT&T might use its monopoly revenues and economic power in the regulated sector to compete unfairly in unregulated markets. The FCC therefore ordered AT&T to provide unregulated services and equipment, including videotext, through an arms-length subsidiary (nicknamed "Baby Bell"). The Commission said other telephone companies could offer these items without restriction, except that to prevent cross-subsidy they had to establish separate accounts for regulated and unregulated items.

The *Computer II* decision is being challenged in court on two grounds: 1) that the Act does not allow the Commission to deregulate on its own and 2) that the decision asserts jurisdiction the FCC does not have in the unregulated data processing field. Congress is working on legislation that generally follows the *Computer II* approach. The Senate has passed a bill, S.898, which would deregulate "information services," a category, similar to enhanced services, that clearly includes videotext. The bill enables AT&T to provide most enhanced services through a separate subsidiary but restricts AT&T's role in videotext content. The House is considering legislation with the same basic structure but much tougher controls on AT&T.

The Justice Department Settlement

The situation changed dramatically in January 1982, when AT&T and the Justice Department announced settlement of their six-year-old antitrust case. If the judge who is presiding over the case approves, their deal will split off the local Bell telephone operating companies from the remainder of AT&T. Effective in late 1983 the local companies will become seven free-standing corporations, each of which will be limited to regulated, local transmission services. The only role for these companies in videotext content will be electronic directory assistance—a computerized *White Pages*.

In return for this surgery, the new decree liberates the remaining part of AT&T from the 1956 decree's restrictions. The company will be free to enter any unregulated field, including videotext services and terminals and also the services that underlie videotext, such as print publishing, retailing and consumer finance. Since this decision cuts through the Gordian Knot that *Computer II* was designed to unravel, the FCC may now create a new set of rules while Congress continues trying to make its own policy.

THE SEPARATIONS ISSUE: SHOULD TELEPHONE COMPANIES BE INFORMATION PROVIDERS?

The FCC's deregulation policy was based on a judgment that enhanced services face vigorous competition. The Commission found that there are "literally thousands" of unregulated computer service vendors offering services through the telephone network, and that the trend is accelerating. Under these circumstances, the Commission saw no reason to keep telephone companies out of the fray. The Commission felt that the carriers would contribute expertise and new products, thereby benefitting consumers and strengthening competition.

Critics of this policy—notably newspaper publishers—have three objections. First, they argue that telephone companies' control of the transmission network gives the carriers an unfair advantage over competitors who must use their facilities. The telephone companies can use their monopoly revenues to subsidize enhanced services, e.g., by charging the cost of shared equipment to the rate-payers. These companies also can design their networks in ways that handicap competitors. These concerns have focused on AT&T because its local operating companies serve 80% of the public and its long distance network dominates the field. The contention is that the arms-length subsidiary required by *Computer II* for AT&T is inadequate to prevent that company from favoring its videotext operation over competitors' systems which must use AT&T lines.

Second, critics argue that competition in electronic publishing is not yet vigorous because this business is just starting. Companies considering this new and risky business could be scared off by telephone companies' competitive advantages.

In addition, some argue that AT&T would acquire excessive political and social power if it were allowed into the information business. If videotext eventually achieves influence comparable to that of newspapers and broadcasting, AT&T's control of the information could mean an unacceptable concentration of power.

Electronic Advertising

Much of the concern about AT&T's role in electronic publishing is generated by the prospect of an "electronic *Yellow Pages.*" The *Yellow Pages* represent the largest publishing venture in the United States, with annual advertising revenues of several billion dollars. As people acquire videotext terminals, telephone companies naturally are interested in moving directory services, such as directory assistance, the *White Pages* and the *Yellow Pages*, to electronic form. In time, this shift should save money on printing and on paying information operators, and it will allow instant updating. The French Telephone Authority thinks the savings will be so great that it is considering installing free directory assistance terminals throughout the country.

The problem is that advertising on an electronic *Yellow Pages* is indistinguishable from other types of advertising. Because such a system would be continuously updated, listings could advertise prices, announce sales and so on. Newspaper and other print publishers who are considering their own electronic publishing ventures would find themselves in direct competition with an electronic *Yellow Pages* operation controlled by the company that also controls the only videotext pipeline to the home.

The antitrust settlement bars the Bell operating companies from non-monopoly businesses, and that presumably includes the *Yellow Pages*. However, there is talk in Congress about reversing this decision, to keep all *Yellow Pages* revenue available to subsidize local telephone rates. Assuming the local operating companies do give up this business, it is not clear whether AT&T or others will take it over. The heart of any *Yellow Pages* operation, whether printed or electronic, is a set of computer tapes listing all the telephone subscribers in an area. The local companies could sell those tapes to the highest bidder or could make them available at a flat charge to anyone who wanted them, creating the possibility of multiple, competing electronic listings. Some form of electronic *Yellow Pages* will be a major factor in videotext, but it is not clear who the publishers will be, or how many.

Policy Proposals

In any case, before the antitrust settlement these concerns persuaded the Senate to adopt a provision in 1981 barring AT&T from providing "mass media" services over its *local* lines. In the House, Communications Subcommittee Chairman Timothy Wirth introduced more restrictive legislation extending the prohibition to all "information publishing," and to long distance lines and barring indirect AT&T involvement in content through joint ventures. Both bills would leave AT&T free to use other media, including print; they focus on the combination of content and monopoly conduit.

Some have questioned the constitutionality of such provisions, since they limit AT&T's freedom of expression, but such legislation probably would be upheld. The Supreme Court has repeatedly sustained federal restrictions on ownership and use of electronic communications when the purpose is diversity and the restrictions are drawn narrowly. For example, the Court has sustained restrictions on newspaper ownership of broadcast stations, and has also upheld the Fairness and Equal Time impositions on broadcasters' freedom.

The more difficult question is whether antitrust legislation is still needed, in view of the settlement. That debate now breaks down into three separate issues:

1. The new consent decree of 1982 restricts the Bell local companies to regulated transmission services, thereby excluding them from providing any videotext services except directory assistance. Sooner or later these companies will demand that this restriction be lifted.

2. The independent telephone companies—which have local monopolies serving 20% of telephone subscribers—are free to provide videotext. Logically, they have the same competitive advantage as the Bell companies, so perhaps they should be treated in the same way.

3. The 1982 decree frees the national AT&T entity to provide videotext. Although there is competition in long distance services,

AT&T still controls the vast bulk of the network. Some argue, therefore, that AT&T should be kept out of electronic publishing over its own lines.

Logically the concern about the Bell operating companies and the independents is the same: control of the local transmission monopoly network gives carriers a competitive advantage over other would-be information providers that must use that network. However, some of the independent telephone companies already have entered the videotext field, and no one is making a serious argument that their threat to competition is severe enough to keep them out. The Bell operating companies are being singled out because of the antitrust sins of the parent, not because their economic situation is different.

Thus, the Bell companies are bound to seek to have the restriction removed. They will argue 1) that their lines remain available to all, 2) that they will not discriminate against competitors, 3) that they are operating videotext computers for directory assistance and could use those machines for other services, and 4) that the different treatment of the dependent companies is unfair. They also will point out that two-way cable is becoming a competitive medium, and they may argue that over-the-air teletext also competes with videotext and should be counted in assessing whether the local exchange actually is a monopoly. Within this decade either the court or the Congress is likely to accept these arguments.

The other separations issue is the role of AT&T. The long distance network will be indispensable to most videotext operators because their local data bases either will include national material (e.g., stock quotes) transmitted to them or will provide "gateways" to switch customers to data bases in distant cities. While competitors are growing rapidly, AT&T still dominates long distance service and has the only lines reaching most towns and rural areas. AT&T's potential advantages over competing electronic publishers include cross-subsidy from regulated transmission revenues (e.g., the cost of a computer used both for transmission and videotext might be placed disproportionately on the former service); discriminatory treatment in connection to the network; and design of the network to favor AT&T's operations (e.g., by building data lines that happen to run to the cities in which AT&T has its videotext computers). For example, information on the length and origin of each incoming call to a data base is useful to a videotext operator. If AT&T gives itself this information it would have to provide it to competitors, but AT&T could design its system to make the data available only in certain locations—i.e., those that coincide with its videotext facilities.

Cross-subsidy and discrimination remain illegal under the Communications Act and could lead to new antitrust prosecutions, so some doubt there is much risk here. Others contend that it would be hard to police the subtle ways that AT&T could place competitors at a disadvantage and that the problem is still a deterrent to entry by potential information providers.

This debate is continuing in Congress. Key Senate leaders have said the local monopoly is the only problem, so that restrictions on AT&T are protectionist and unnecessary. Representative Wirth and the newspaper publishers say AT&T should be kept out of videotext content until long distance transmission is truly competitive. Wirth's subcommittee has adopted a bill that bars both AT&T and the Bell operating companies from providing content over their own lines, while returning the printed *Yellow Pages* to the operating companies and allowing them into videotext whenever alternative local transmission facilities become available. The argument will continue while Congress debates legislation, but the case for restrictions will be weakened as transmission competition increases. If there is no legislation, the FCC is unlikely to act, so AT&T will be free to enter any videotext arena on an unregulated basis.

ACCESS TO THE NETWORKS— VIDEOTEXT PROVIDED BY NON-CARRIERS

While the public debate has focused on the separations question, the issue of a right of access also bears heavily on the prospects for videotext. The regulated telephone network—both local and national—is, of course, open to access by all. The essence of common carrier regulation is that anyone can use the facility, under nondiscriminatory rates and terms. However, under *Computer II* this policy does not apply to "enhanced" networks, such as high-speed data networks that link computers and manipulate the information along the way or to the data base computers themselves. In addition, there is a consensus in Congress that any new communications legislation should provide for eventual deregulation of long distance transmission on competitive routes.

These policy changes will not affect regular telephone service for many years, but they will affect electronic publishers that wish to use long distance specialized data networks. In time, such publishers may have to depend on unregulated networks, without rate regulation or any automatic right of access. The practical effect of this trend will depend on the number of available competing networks. In view of the rapid growth in satellite services and microwave links, there probably will be vigorous competition on high-volume routes linking major cities. Operators wishing to reach small centers may find fewer choices, higher prices and perhaps discriminatory treatment.

Another access issue involves the provision of calling number identification and billing information by the local telephone companies. This data is now automatically transmitted to AT&T for long distance calls. If electronic publishers selling subscription services can get this information, their billing task will be greatly simplified. The proposed consent decree is unclear, however, on whether the Bell operating companies must provide it.

Access to Computer Space

During the 1980s AT&T and the other carriers will be installing large computers to handle directory services, electronic mail and message storage. Such facilities also can be used as videotext gateways, and for storage and retrieval of videotext messages provided by other publishers. For example , if telephone subscribers become accustomed to dialing a certain number to reach a telephone company computer and retrieve any messages, it should be easy to get them to use the same system to obtain information, order tickets and so on.

Because videotext is to be an unregulated service, telephone and other companies operating data bases have no obligation to make computer space available to other information providers. Legislation could change this situation for AT&T, requiring the company to make available to all electronic publishers space on computers used for videotext services, on nondiscriminatory terms. This policy offers the smallest potential publisher the opportunity to reach the public without the necessity of making a huge investment in a company computer. In addition, it would ensure that the range of videotext services available to the public would include a kind of "community bulletin board," which anyone could dial up to post notices or to read them.

The AT&T settlement, however, may have derailed this approach. The Bell operating companies will have computers to manage basic communications services—including electronic directory assistance—

but the new consent decree forbids them from using those computers for any other purpose. The independent telephone companies and AT&T will be free to run videotext computers, but the decree places them under no obligation to make access available to others. The Wirth bill would create such an obligation, but it is less likely to be preserved in the final legislation—if there is any—because of the perception that there is less need for regulatory intervention.

In theory, if many potential publishers are willing to pay for time on someone else's data base, videotext operators will emerge to set up computers on a "carrier" basis and provide access to all. Unlike transmission, no government permission is required to set up a computer, and there is no evidence that economies of scale will create a monopoly or oligopoly in this field. In reality , however, even if there is a demand for such services, they may take a long time to develop. Videotext providers will most likely wish to retain control over the information in their data bases, both to keep users happy and to avoid possible liability for defamatory or obscene material. It will take years of litigation to decide whether a system operator that provides such access voluntarily is a publisher—and thus fully liable for content—or a "carrier" that can avoid liability.

On the other hand, any attempt to mandate access would create serious problems. A requirement of reasonable access would lead to government oversight of the rates being charged. In the end, all the travails of traditional economic regulation could land on the heretofore unregulated data processing business. The problems would be particularly severe because the carrier would be using the computer to publish its own information as well as that of other information providers; regulators would face endless disputes over whether the carrier is discriminating in its own favor. Without evidence both that the demand for data base capacity exists and that the market will not meet it, these problems outweigh the speculative benefits of mandatory access. However, as will be discussed in Chapter 10, policies that give videotext operators the *option* of acting as carriers—by avoiding content liability—would be in everyone's interest.

Antitrust Law

Without legislation, the one other possible source of a right of access comes from antitrust law. There is a "bottleneck" theory of monopolization, which holds that "a business or group of businesses in control of a scarce facility have an obligation to give competitors reasonable access"[4] when the facility is essential to the business. This doctrine reinforces the right of access to the telephone network, but court-ordered access to a data base is unlikely. Computer storage and retrieval may be costly, but they are not scarce. There are multiple facilities now, and there will be many more. Neither regulation nor technology limits the number of videotext data bases, and economics is not likely to make any individual computer "essential" enough to make it the kind of bottleneck that has prompted court action.

RATE REGULATION

In addition to the question of whether carriers will be allowed to provide the videotext content, there is the question of how they will be regulated. *Computer II* says that the FCC will not regulate the videotext service itself, but potential electronic publishers must also consider what they will pay for transmission.

At present, the FCC oversees all sales of interstate transmission services; carriers must file tariffs specifying the rates and the nature of the service to be provided. However, recent FCC decisions have eliminated serious regulatory scrutiny for carriers that lack market power. Thus, independent carriers such as MCI or Tymnet can change their tariffs with little fear that the FCC will overrule them. The Commission does still control the rates satellite carriers charge, although it is moving to free them. The one remaining area of full rate-of-return regulation is AT&T's long distance network. Bell still controls about 95% of the nation's long distance traffic, so the FCC feels competition is not yet strong enough to justify loosened controls.

State Regulation

At the state level, regulation affects rates, and it may extend to information services. The Communications Act gives the states exclusive jurisdiction over charges and practices for "intrastate communication service by wire or radio of any carrier."[5] Thus, when a videotext user calls a data base in the same state, the state regulates the transmission charge.

The manner in which local telephone rates are regulated will have great impact on the development of telephone videotext services. Most experts see heavy pressure on local rates during the 1980s because of inflation, the need to write off old equipment and the loss of subsidies that have been built into the cost accounting for equipment shared by local and toll services. State regulators are likely to offset these pressures by slapping stiff "access charges" on all long distance carriers that connect to local exchanges. The higher these charges, the more expensive it will be to use data bases that are located out of town, and the more reason electronic publishers will have to set up data bases in individual cities instead of on a regional or national basis. Because non-local information will be essential to most videotext services, operators may seek to avoid excess charges by bringing in updates over private satellite circuits and storing them in their computers for retrieval by customers, rather than using a "gateway" system that interconnects local and long distance circuits.

In addition, many states will move to "usage sensitive pricing" for local rates. Under this approach the customer is charged for each minute of network use; this is justified because heavy users are responsible for a large share of the cost of building and maintaining the system, especially those who use the network during peak daytime hours. Because videotext may involve many minutes or even hours of transmission per day, usage sensitive pricing will drive some users away from the telephone network and toward cable or over-the-air transmission.

While state regulation of transmission rates now exists and will continue, regulation of intrastate information services—e.g., control over the price an electronic publisher charges per page—is uncertain. There is no such regulation of videotext today, but states do regulate the charges telephone companies set for such information services as dial-up time or weather. State authority to impose such controls on videotext depends on each state's public utility law. In general, state regulators may be able to force telephone companies to file tariffs for their videotext offerings, but such controls are unlikely for other companies. At the moment, the issue of state control applies only to the independent telephone companies (e.g., GTE and Continental), because the new consent decree keeps the Bell operating companies out of videotext. Carriers that do provide videotext may be able to avoid state regulation by designing transmission facilities that route all the messages out of state and back in. Nevertheless, some carriers are likely to provide local information to local users through local lines and could be affected by state controls.

FCC Preemption

If state regulators do try to regulate carriers' information rates, they will run into possible FCC preemption of their authority. *Computer II* explicitly preempted state controls on equipment, but it was silent on enhanced services. When the Commission wrote this decision the staff considered making explicit the preemption of enhanced services, but they decided not to add that controversy to an already complex proceeding. The Commission is likely to assert preemption when an appropriate case comes up. However, it may not be able to enforce that policy.

As Washington has pushed for competition and deregulation over the past decade, it had a string of fights with the states over preemption. A series of court decisions has held that the FCC can win on preemption if it can show that state regulation would seriously impede legitimate national policies. For example, the FCC won when it preempted state controls on telephone equipment in order to let competitors into the business.[6]

In the case of videotext, preemption is a close question. State regulation of intrastate information rates could distort development of the national videotext business by inducing operators to avoid providing local service or by pushing them to build extra lines that cross state borders. However, similar arguments could be made against state regulation of transmission rates, under which the telephone system has survived and even prospered. A court test probably would turn on the practical effects of a state's regulatory program in a particular case.

State regulation of information rates is a poor idea, for the reasons discussed in Chapter 4. Failing a clear decision by the FCC and the Courts, Congress can and should settle the matter by preempting the area.

CONCLUSION

Whether legislation passes or not, *Computer II* and the antitrust settlement have cleared away most of the fog. Telephone videotext probably will operate as follows:

- AT&T will sell equipment and long distance transmission, and it may be able to provide content as well, depending on what Congress does.

- The Bell operating companies will be limited to transmission and excluded from videotext content for a few years but eventually will be freed to do anything.

- All others, including the independent telephone companies, will be free to enter any part of the videotext business.

- Electronic publishers will have a right of access to the basic transmission network but not to data bases or to sophisticated data networks.

- There will be no other regulation of telephone videotext, except for rate regulation of the underlying transmission service and possible regulation in a few states of the rates telephone companies charge for local information.

FOOTNOTES

1. 47 U.S.C. § 223.
2. 13 U.S.C. § 1335.
3. 77 F.C.C.2d 384.
4. *Byars v. Bluff City News Co., Inc.*, 609 F.2d 843 (6th Cir., 1979).
5. 47 U.S.C. § 152(b).
6. *North Carolina Utilities Commission v. FCC*, 537 F. 2d 787 (4th Cir., 1976).

7

Electronic Publishing Over Cable TV

Current regulations governing cable television affect content, rates and structure. Since they are imposed by federal, state and local authorities, and are in the midst of fundamental transition, cable transmission of teletext and videotext presents especially complex issues. This chapter will summarize existing cable policies and then describe how those policies affect electronic publishing and how they might be changed.

OVERALL REGULATORY SCHEME FOR CABLE

Cable began as a way to improve reception of television signals, and the FCC asserted jurisdiction on the basis that cable is "ancillary" to broadcasting.[1] The Commission adopted a comprehensive regulatory program in 1972. The FCC's approach was based on the Communications Act's broadcasting title, but it included many arrangements specially designed for cable. Court and FCC decisions dismantled most of those controls in the second half of the 1970s, but the Commission still imposes content regulations and a few restrictions on retransmission of over-the-air programs.

Some states have cable legislation, but the most significant regulations are imposed by local authorities. Cable operators need a "franchise" to run their wires through the streets, and many cities have adopted controls on rates, access, ownership and system design as a condition for granting a franchise.

Content Regulation

The Communications Act's content provisions have only one reference to cable TV: they say cable is to be treated as a broadcast station for purposes of Section 315.[2] This section includes the Fairness Doctrine, the Equal Time Rule and the requirement that advertising sold to a political candidate be at the lowest unit rate. Congress adopted the cable language in 1971 as part of a broader bill intended to control the cost of campaigning. Legislative history indicates Congress gave no thought to the general question of cable content.[3] The 1971 law appeared to include cable under the section that gives political candidates the right to buy broadcast time,[4] but a subsequent amendment has been interpreted as deleting that provision. The only other applicable statutory provision is the ban on cigarette advertising.[5]

The FCC has issued regulations that incorporate the statutory requirements and a few other broadcast-type rules, such as the requirement that advertisements be identified. However, the Commission's rules apply only to "origination cablecasting," programming controlled by the cable operator. There is an exemption for "access channels," which are controlled by local governments, schools, the general public and others. The FCC's 1972 rules required cable operators to provide access channels and forbade the operators from censoring them. The courts later struck down the FCC's access requirement, but most local authorities have preserved it through the franchise process. Because the cable operator does not control the access channels, the FCC did not want to hold the operator responsible for their content.

The law, however, makes no distinction between origination and access channels, so the rule's legality is unclear. The Commission did say in a 1980 decision that the political and fairness rules would not apply to access programming "as long as the channels on which such programming is presented themselves have, inherent in their functioning, access of a type which makes possible equal opportunities for political candidates and time for the provision of programming covering all sides of controversial issues of public importance." The quite sensible idea is to determine whether the overall cable operation meets the goals of Equal Time and Fairness, rather than impose those rules rigidly on a channel-by-channel basis. However, this vague policy has never been interpreted or applied, so it is difficult to know how a particular Fairness complaint about an access channel would be handled.

The issue is further confused because the evolution of the cable industry has obscured the dividing line between "origination" and "access." Many cable systems now take packages of programming from satellites and distribute them to subscribers (on a "pay" or "free" basis) without alteration. It is unclear whether such services are "origination" or "access"; the answer may depend on the details of the cable operator's contract with the program supplier. This area remains foggy because there have been few complaints about cable content in the past, but disputes are bound to come as cable service grows. Political disputes will be handled by the FCC, while complaints about obscene programming are likely to go to local franchise authorities and the courts.

Economic Regulation

The FCC has never regulated the rates that cable subscribers are charged, but economic regulation is a strong force at the local level. Cable operators typically make commitments on initial rates for basic and pay services during the franchise process. The FCC has preempted ongoing rate regulation for "pay" channels, but many cities do rule on operators' requests for rate hikes for basic service.

Structural Regulation

The courts struck down the FCC's access channel requirements because they exceeded the Commission's "ancillary" jurisdiction and imposed common carrier obligations on a broadcast-type service, in violation of the Communications Act.[6] The FCC probably could develop a new jurisdictional theory to support an access requirement, but such an adventure seems unlikely because of the current antiregulatory mood in Washington and the tradition of regulation and litigation under the "ancillary" theory. The FCC's only remaining structural requirement is the "must carry" rule, which requires cable operators to carry certain local television signals.[7]

TELETEXT AND VIDEOTEXT ON CABLE— CONTENT REGULATION

The rules governing cable have no specific provisions for electronic publishing. The general rules are vague enough, but extrapolating them to teletext and videotext is particularly difficult because those services may not fall under the rubric of "cable television."

The FCC's authority over cable is limited to areas "ancillary to broadcasting," and the Commission itself has said that teletext is not "broadcasting." In addition, the rules were written for TV "programming," and that term arguably does not apply here. If the FCC's rules do apply, the Commission clearly has the authority to drop them.

This conclusion avoids what would otherwise be the frustrating task of trying to fit information services into "origination" and "access" pigeonholes. For example, if a cable operator has a long term contract with *The New York Times* to put the newspaper in a videotext data base, the operator does not have control, so the content rules presumably would not apply. However, the answer may change if the cable operator has the right to change the paper's format to fit the computer program, or if the operator decides which stories to use or rewrites them. The FCC has no business evaluating individual contracts to draw these distinctions. Courts may have to do so to deal with defamation and obscenity, as discussed in Chapter 10, but there is no reason to duplicate that effort or run the risk of creating two inconsistent policies.

Unfortunately, this approach leaves the FCC in the messy business of distinguishing between video and electronic publishing. That line will be hard to draw for broadcasting and even harder for cable. The full channel teletext services likely on cable will be able to present animation and still photographs, features often seen on regular video channels. Moreover, cable operators may provide videotext services such as one that allows a subscriber interested in buying a house to dial up a video tape of the house together with a text description. Attempts to fit such services into "electronic publishing" and "television programming" pigeonholes would be frustrating and, in the end, futile.

Moreover, whatever the FCC does with its own rules, the Act still applies. If Fairness and Equal Time apply by law to broadcast teletext— and they may, as Chapter 5 indicated—then Section 315 applies them to electronic publishing on cable.

The only final answer is new legislation that sets sensible rules for all cable services. As argued in Chapter 4, the Equal Time rule should be retained for paid political advertising—if a cable operator or an individual channel programmer takes ads from one candidate, then ads should be taken from all other candidates. The other content rules should be eliminated, freeing cable to provide the full diversity that its technology makes possible.

FEDERAL PREEMPTION OF STATE AND LOCAL REGULATION

While the federal content issues remain complex, the federal government is otherwise withdrawing from cable regulation. State and local controls now pose the key policy issues. The rules they set can affect content, the rates for information services and the rates for the underlying transmission (i.e., the charge for use or lease of a cable channel).

In the content area, some jurisdictions have written obscenity restrictions into their franchises and at least one state (Utah) has passed a cable obscenity law that a federal court struck down on First Amendment grounds. Other kinds of content rules have so far been left to the FCC but may appear as the Commission vacates the field. Observers anticipate a surge of state and local attempts to restrict obscenity in response to increased offerings of "adult" programming. The consequences for electronic publishers are discussed in Chapter 10.

As for rate controls, they may be imposed through state common carrier regulation, local regulation or city-cable agreements made during the franchise process. Electronic publishing is too new for anyone to be regulating information rates, although the possibility must be assessed. State and local regulation of transmission rates already is a hot topic in cable policy.

The power of non-federal authorities to regulate in these areas depends upon the amount of the terrain preempted by Washington. The FCC's 1972 rules attempted to preempt content and rate regulation except for rate controls on the "basic" cable package provided to all subscribers. The Commission argued that regulation would inhibit innovative uses of channels; that harm to one kind of cable service would harm others because cable is a single economic entity; and that the Commission's cable policy was integral to its overall broadcasting policy.

There have been two important court tests of this policy. The FCC was upheld on the issue of the rates charged subscribers for "pay" television.[8] This decision affirmed the FCC's judgment that common-carrier-type controls would have a "chilling effect" on new services, harming its policy of encouraging diversity through the development of pay television services.

The Commission lost, however, when the issue was regulation of transmission rates for intrastate, two-way, point-to-point, "non-video" signals.[9] The court said such services are not "ancillary to broadcasting"

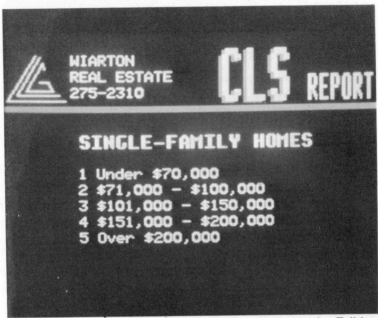

The shop-at-home house hunter presses buttons on the Telidon videotext controller to obtain information on single family homes. Five price categories appear on the screen.

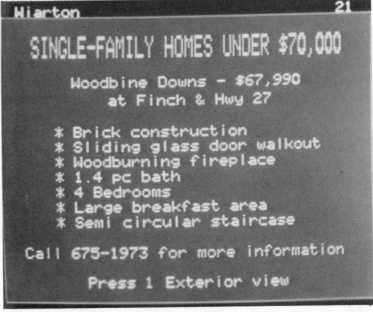

After choosing the "under $70,000" price category, the shopper is provided with a list of specific features.

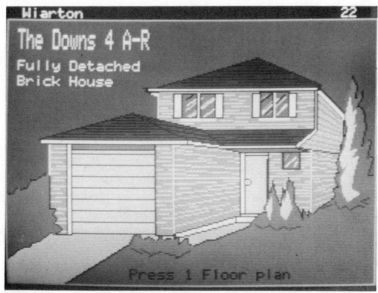

If the shopper requires more information, a graphic picture of the house can be shown.

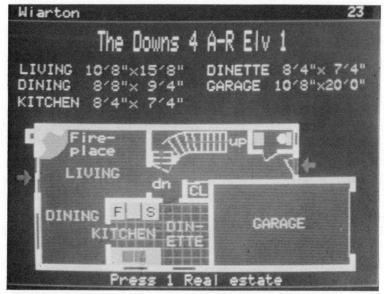

Further details, such as room dimensions and a floor plan, can also be provided. All photos courtesy of Telidon.

and therefore fall under Section 2(b) of the Communications Act, which bars FCC control over the charges for "intrastate communications." The key to this decision was the lack of evidence supporting the FCC's claim that "its long term communications goals will be impaired if two-way, non-video communications over leased access channels are subject to state or local common carrier regulation."

Criteria for Preemption

These cases suggest three criteria to analyze any particular cable preemption issue: 1) whether the service is ancillary to broadcasting; 2) whether the non-federal regulation falls under Section 2(b) of the Act; and 3) whether as a practical matter the non-federal regulation would disrupt a legitimate FCC policy.

The first two criteria suggest that the Commission's preemption authority is stronger for teletext than videotext. Teletext seems to be more "ancillary" because it will appear on regular broadcast stations, and its one-way nature means that it is not the kind of common carrier-type service that Section 2(b) covers. However, this is a senseless way to set the rules. Teletext and videotext on cable are likely to perform many of the same functions; system operators may switch back and forth from one to the other; and there are middle-ground technologies that blur the dividing line. For example, a cable information system may work by sending electronic pages downstream in response to customers' requests transmitted upstream through the telephone network. The scope of state and local authority should not depend on whether such a service is classified as "teletext" or "videotext."

Fortunately, the two court decisions essentially turned on the third criterion: whether enforcement of the non-federal rule would seriously impair a legitimate national policy. Under this approach, teletext and videotext can be treated uniformly because they both provide information services to the public throughout the nation—a well-established goal of broadcasting policy. Therefore, the FCC's ability to preempt will depend on the particular situation.

Content is the Commission's strongest ground. Section 2(b) does not apply here, and the Commission can make a strong case that the growth of cable services would be hampered by non-federal content controls. Nevertheless, state and local rules that are constitutional and apply to the media in general—such as defamation and obscenity laws—fall within a long-standing area of state authority, are unlikely to disrupt national

TRACK 2 BLUE PAGES   31131017a   op

TRACK 2
ADULT ENTERTAINMENT

ADULT ENTERTAINMENT
1.Experience Sauna
2.Massage Parlours
3.Stud Bookshops
4.Escort Agencies
5.The Venus Room
6.S & M Holdings, Ltd.
7.Archer Cinema
8.Louise Solomon

0 FOR ALPHABETICAL INDEX 'A'

Frames such as this one appear on Prestel's videotext system, but may be restricted in the United States due to efforts of state and local authorities. Artist's drawing of Prestel frame, based on photograph supplied courtesy of Prestel.

services, and almost certainly are not preempted in their application to cable. By contrast, Congress has explicitly covered the area of political content, so non-federal action there probably would be thrown out.

Rate Regulation

Intrastate information rates may well be preemptable, but the FCC would have to prove that non-federal regulation would cause harm. The problems the Commission might try to demonstrate include disincentives for cable operators to offer information services, artificially low prices that limit services, and inefficient cross-subsidies from one part of a service to another. These effects are similar to those the FCC would have to show to sustain preemption of state regulation of "enhanced" telecommunications services under *Computer II*.

The third kind of regulation—control of the rates cable operators charge for providing intrastate transmission—is the weakest area for preemption, because it falls under Section 2(b). Disputes already are underway in several states over whether a cable operator is subjected to state public utility regulation by leasing channels to others, and the answer will depend on individual state laws as well as FCC policies. Because cable transmission may be used for many services, this issue goes beyond electronic publishing.

For all three areas, the situation is confused because the Commission has not stated whether its original, broad preemption claim still stands, now that most of the affirmative requirements in the 1972 rules have been dismantled. One may argue that the Commission has handed cable policy to non-federal authorities and withdrawn from the field. At this point, Congressional action is the only certain way to set the limits on state or local controls.

STRUCTURAL REGULATION—
MANDATORY CHANNEL LEASING

The premise for precluding content and rate regulation is that electronic publishing will be highly competitive. In the case of cable, structural intervention may be needed to realize that potential.

While many cable franchises technically are "non-exclusive," hardly any cities grant franchises to more than one company. In any case, once one company wires an area, no one else is likely to invest the vast sums needed to string parallel cables; thus, cable operators have *de facto* monopolies. This power raises the specters of excessive rates, discrimination against competing content originators and limits on the information available to the public.

Concern about this kind of power has led to calls for a "separations" policy (meaning the cable operator controls only transmission and must take all the content from others) or access (meaning that the cable operator must turn over some channels to others). The FCC's 1972 rules adopted the access approach. Now that those rules have been struck down, the issue is in the hands of the local franchise authorities. No one uses separations; access policies vary throughout the country. A 1981 survey by the National Cable Television Association identified 1018 access channels, most of which fall into three categories of usage: individuals, municipal governments and educational institutions.

Some franchises also follow the general requirement in the old FCC rules that at least one channel be available for lease. This is to ensure diversity in the sources of information and competition among commercial cable services. However, such provisions usually leave cable operators free to decide how many channels will be leased, who gets them and how much to charge. This arrangement allows operators to lease to those who pose the least competitive threat or charge rates so high that competition is impossible. A simple lease requirement standing alone may have little practical effect.

As a result, some experts have proposed more elaborate "mandatory channel leasing" rules. The idea is that government should reserve a fixed number of channels for leases, and regulate the decisions on who may lease and for how much. This approach would make the whole cable system competitive because the cable operator would have to price his own services to meet the competition on the leased channels. If regulation is needed at all, mandatory leasing is a better approach than content regulation because it promotes diversity in the sources of information without putting the government in the position of reviewing content. It is better than rate regulation because it prevents monopoly pricing while leaving most of the channels unregulated.

Arguments Against Mandatory Leasing

While the cable industry generally accepts public access channels, it has several serious and legitimate objections to mandatory leasing. First, the industry contends that the huge investments required to build modern cable systems can be justified only if the cable operator retains control of the income-producing channels. In particular, operators plan on pay television as a major revenue source; they might be severely and unfairly damaged if programmers could lease their own channels and stop sharing profits with the operators. This objection is particularly powerful if the requirement is imposed after the operator has built the system.

Second, by reducing revenues and increasing costs, mandatory leasing could force operators to build smaller or less sophisticated systems than they otherwise would. Alternatively, operators might inflate rates for basic cable services to recover lost revenues.

Third, cable operators are concerned that the public will not understand the concept and will erroneously blame the operators for distasteful content or inefficient services that the operators cannot control.

Fourth, the industry argues that leasing might drag them under state common carrier regulation. Such controls would add a costly and stifling layer of regulation.

These arguments are powerful, but they are not decisive. If cable is going to have true monopoly power, especially over key sources of information, then the public's need for diversity and competition should outweigh the economic burdens of mandatory leasing. Thus, the debate actually turns on the industry's final argument—that cable is not a monopoly because the services it provides compete with other media. In the same way that a newspaper in a one-newspaper town faces competition from other publications, radio and television, the industry points out that it vies for consumers' dollars and attention with broadcasters, newspapers, movie theaters and so on.

From the legal viewpoint, this debate often is couched in terms of models—whether cable is more analogous to broadcasting (which may be regulated) or to print (which may not). From an economic viewpoint, the issue focuses on whether cable has such powerful advantages over other media that it can generate monopoly profits.

The constitutional issue is unsettled. The Supreme Court said in a footnote to a 1978 decision that cable's First Amendment claims are "not frivolous."[10] In 1981 the National Cable Television Association circulated an elaborate analysis arguing that cable is a "telepublisher." The Association argued that the government cannot force newspapers to lease out individual pages, so it should not be able to require cable operators to lease channels.

On the other hand, the one Court of Appeals that has confronted this issue rejected the industry's argument.[11] That decision held that each communications medium is unique, and the First Amendment analysis of cable should take cable's *de facto* monopoly into account. The judges held that the considerations that make content regulation and ownership restrictions permissible for broadcasting—scarcity of outlets, the government's role in awarding them and the public's interest in diversity—do apply to cable. This case did not deal with mandatory leasing, but the theory—that the public's right to multiple voices justifies reasonable government controls—seems to apply to leased channel requirements.

The Problem of Monopoly Power

In any case, these arguments by analogy do not resolve the key issue: whether cable truly does have monopoly power. The answer requires an analysis of market definitions and product costs for the various services cable will provide. Such an analysis is complicated by a shortage of data and a constantly changing technology.

Electronic publishing is, of course, only one of the relevant cable businesses, but its prospects suggest the difficulty of this inquiry. In the teletext area, VBI teletext can provide plenty of competition among narrowband services, but cable's ability to put 5000 pages on each of several dedicated channels swamps the few hundred pages on each television station. On the other hand, broadcasting reaches more people, and it is not clear how many pages per service people will want.

As for videotext, cable currently lags far behind the telephone network. Cable operators are only just beginning to build systems capable of handling two-way services. The telephone network reaches four times as many people as cable, is two-way and has sophisticated switching capability. On the other hand, cable has long-term advantages. All cable systems install terminals in homes, and it is relatively easy to add videotext capacity to those terminals. Cable has greater bandwidth than telephone lines, allowing faster responses, more elegant graphics, and—in time—photographic pages. To complicate the situation further, cable's advantages may be offset by advances in the telephone network, such as the introduction of optical fiber.

It is simply too early to know how much economic power cable will have in electronic publishing. For now, a reasonable guess is that cable will not have a total monopoly in any market, but it will have a powerful position. If a cable system originates all electronic publishing content itself or signs an exclusive contract with one information provider (e.g., a newspaper), competing providers will suffer a true handicap, even though other transmission options would be available. The threat to diversity is heightened by the increasing vertical integration in cable; a company that is both a publisher and a system operator may be tempted to exclude other publishers from its channels.

Diversity in control of the sources of information is so important that it is worth taking some risks to protect it, particularly if, as suggested, there are to be no content or rate regulations. The best policy for now is to keep the option open and for local authorities to experiment with mandatory leasing. Practical experience in individual communities would greatly help an understanding of cable's power and the formation of national policy.

Mandatory leasing is most appropriate for systems with large numbers of channels. Those systems have the greatest long-term competitive advantages, and small systems (e.g., those with 12 channels) have no excess capacity available for lease. Of course, many franchises already have been awarded, but local policymakers will have a second chance when franchises come up for renewal, especially because many old cable systems will be rebuilding to increase capacity.

Policy Complications

Cities that do try mandatory leasing must deal with myriad practical problems. For example, policymakers should avoid allocating the leased channels to specific services, such as videotext. A city would face huge problems in trying to define all the services that might use leased channels and set priorities for them, and such decisions would have to be changed frequently. If lessees are given the freedom to decide how to use their channels or to sublease them, the market should push channel uses toward the greatest consumer demands. Under this arrangement, leased channels will be used for electronic publishing if services on other media and the operators' own channels fail to meet consumers' demands or are overpriced. In other words, this arrangement would promote diversity and competition without wasting channel capacity on services no one wants. However, practical economics may make it necessary to exclude pay TV from leasing.

A tougher problem is settling the lease charge without creating a regulatory morass. One option is to auction off the leased channels. Another is to turn them over to a third party—e.g., a board that represents the city—and let it negotiate the rates. Arbitration is a third possibility, and a fourth is to require that the charge be "reasonable" and leave the specifics to negotiation or litigation between the cable operator and the lessee. In any case, traditional rate-of-return regulation should be avoided. It would be difficult to verify the costs of system construction in allocating a share to the leased channels or to set a "fair" return on cable investments.

Mandatory leasing involves other issues, such as whether the leased channels should be included in the "basic" service or added as "tiers" for subscribers who want them, how many channels should be included in the requirement, and how long the lease period should be. It will be difficult to design procedures that are fair to cable operators and do not impose a burdensome regulatory process. Policymakers badly need academic analysis of all these issues as well as practical experience.

It should be added that cable operators can act on their own to promote diversity and dilute the case for mandatory leased access. Operators can and should voluntarily lease channels at fair rates while also offering access to their own teletext and videotext data bases.

In fact, many cable operators are eager to cooperate with other information providers because they need material to fill their channels. Ironically, the current confusion about state rate regulation may discourage such voluntary leases. As discussed above, lease of a cable channel may subject the operator to regulation as a common carrier—a status that both city officials and cable operators want to avoid. Therefore, many cable operators insist on joint ventures—and on retaining content control—and refuse to lease. As a result, voluntary leasing—and diversity—might be increased if Congress were to preempt state regulation of cable transmission rates.

If there is no mandatory leased access and the cable operator refuses to lease voluntarily, a potential cable user might try a "bottleneck" antitrust argument similar to that discussed earlier for telephone videotext data bases. Such an argument might succeed if cable was a unique and indispensable transmission medium. At present, however, cable's advantages probably do not add up to the kind of monopoly power that would lead a court to order access. In any case, a cable operator probably can defeat such a claim if he can show that his channels are fully utilized.

THE "MUST-CARRY" RULE

The FCC's "must-carry" rule raises a final, special access issue. This rule requires cable operators to carry certain local over-the-air television stations. It is imposed to ensure that cable subscribers can receive local programs and to protect local stations against loss of audiences.

The Commission recently held that this requirement does not apply to pay-TV stations, on the grounds that pay services can fend for themselves in the marketplace. Subscriber VBI teletext logically should not be covered for the same reason.

The must-carry rule is an old battleground between broadcasters and cable. Broadcasters argue that local television service is important to communities, and the audience could disappear if cable subscribers do not receive local stations, especially because cable installers often disconnect television antennas. Cable operators answer that the market should rule: they should be allowed to use their channels for whatever programs the audience demands, without regulatory interference.

Whatever the merits of this debate for television, there is no need for similar protection for teletext. There is no existing, locally oriented teletext service to protect, and cable is as likely to start a service as is broadcasting. Cable operators should be free to run TV stations' VBI services or to strip those signals and insert their own. As discussed in Chapter 11 the courts might decide that in a few cases simultaneous teletext and television programs comprise a single work for copyright purposes. In that event, the cable operator would have to run the teletext. That is a copyright issue, however, and does not require FCC intervention.

FOOTNOTES

1. The Supreme Court upheld this theory in *U.S. v. Southeastern Cable Co.*, 392 U.S. 157 (1968).
2. 47 U.S.C. 315(c).
3. See "Cable Television and the Political Broadcasting Laws: the 1980 Election Experience and Proposals for Change." FCC Cable Television Bureau, January, 1981.

4. 47 U.S.C. 312(a)(7).

5. 13 U.S.C. 1335.

6. *Midwest Video v. FCC,* 440 U.S. 689 (1979).

7. 47 C.F.R. §§ 76.55-63.

8. *Brookhaven Cable TV, Inc. v. Kelly,* 573 F.2d 763 (2nd Cir., 1978).

9. *National Association of Regulatory Utility Commissioners v. FCC,* 533 F.2d 601 (D.C. Cir., 1976).

10. *Midwest Video v. FCC,* 440 U.S. 698 (1979).

11. *Community Communications Co. v. City of Boulder* ("Boulder II"), 630 F.2d 3704 (1981).

8
Technical Standards

Of all the issues raised by electronic publishing, the one that has received the most attention so far is the need for technical standards. The stakes here are substantial—national pride, large investments and the speed and direction of the industry's growth. For these reasons, the standards issue has escalated from engineering seminars to an all-out diplomatic and marketing war.

This issue involves both teletext and videotext. Because broadcast teletext uses over-the-air frequencies, formal FCC authorization is needed to begin regular service. When the FCC provides that authorization, it must decide what, if any, standards to set. There is nothing new about this process; the Commission has set standards for radio, television and many other new broadcast services through the years.

Videotext and cable teletext, by contrast, do not need FCC approval to begin operations. The FCC has no interest in setting standards for these wireline services, and it may lack power to do so. However, teletext and videotext will use some of the same microprocessors, and many electronic publishers will want to use both distribution media for their data bases. Therefore, decisions in one area affect the other.

The FCC is not the only forum for the standards debate. Two private industry groups in the United States, the Electronic Industries Association (EIA) and the American National Standards Institute (ANSI), are studying this issue. These groups make their decisions by consensus, however, and they are deeply split at present.

An international standards-setting process is also underway. The Consultative Committee on International Telephony and Telegraphy (CCITT), a unit of the International Telecommunications Union (ITU) which administers worldwide telephone standards, has begun a long term project to develop a videotext standard. If the CCITT succeeds in this effort, the decision would not legally bind U.S. companies, although it might have some psychological impact.

In sum, without FCC action the standards decision will be up to three groups of individual companies: terminal manufacturers (and the microprocessor producers that supply parts for the terminals); transmission networks; and data base publishers. The current difficulty is that each of these groups needs the others to make the business work, and each company is afraid to pick a standard first for fear that it will end up riding the wrong horse.

The key standards issue is how to code the digital signals that teletext and videotext transmit to represent letters, numbers, designs, colors and so on. A language is needed to permit terminals to "understand" data bases. In addition to this "presentation level" standard, there are important but less controversial decisions to be made on transmission issues, such as which vertical blanking interval (VBI) lines should be used and how fast the data should be sent. The decisions on the various standards issues will determine how terminals are built and what data bases they can receive, so they will have a great impact on two factors that are critical to the growth of electronic publishing: terminal cost and system compatibility.

BACKGROUND

The debate over the presentation level began with three incompatible systems that had been developed with government sponsorship: Prestel/Ceefax (British), Antiope (French) and Telidon (Canadian). Salesmen for these systems began showing their wares in the United States in 1979. In 1980 the Columbia Broadcasting System (CBS) asked the FCC to adopt Antiope as the broadcast teletext presentation standard and proposed a transmission scheme. In early 1981 the British submitted a paper criticizing the French system and proposing their own.

In May 1981 CBS and the French joined with AT&T and the Canadians to announce a new presentation standard that incorporated Antiope and Telidon features, as well as some AT&T innovations. The new allies called their proposal the "North American Standard."

However, this agreement leaves manufacturers enough options on terminal design choices that development of incompatible terminals is still possible. In addition, the British have kept their own system, and they have attracted some adherents among U.S. broadcasters, notably the Field and Taft broadcasting groups.

In November 1981, the FCC held a meeting on teletext standards. After a brief debate, the Commissioners proposed that the market, not the government, should make the decision. Consistent with Washington's current passion for deregulation, they proposed rules calling for an "open environment policy," which allows each broadcaster to make the decision on which system to use.[1] Under this approach, a variety of incompatible systems may be adopted. The Commission proposed standards limited to transmission issues; it stated that it would regulate only where necessary to prevent interference with regular TV signals.

While the Canadian Government adopted the North American Standard for its teletext and videotext services, the French and British worked out a compromise videotext presentation standard that differs substantially from the North American Standard called the "CEPT (Européan des Postes et Téléphones) Standard," after the organization of Western European telecommunications authorities. The individual European countries are keeping their different teletext standards, apparently because they contemplate substantial information flows across borders by wire but not by broadcast media.

The CCITT is examining compromises between the North American and CEPT Standards, but manufacturers and data base providers on both continents are committing too much money to make further change easy. Development of a single, worldwide standard therefore looks unlikely, and agreement on a single U.S. system is uncertain as well.

AT&T has responded to this situation by proposing a "session level" standard that would let a videotext computer query a terminal concerning which standard it uses and then send appropriately formatted information. This compromise would allow otherwise incompatible systems to communicate, and it might be practical for some high-value data bases, such as those that would be involved in transatlantic videotext services. However, this approach would be too costly to be a general solution for the domestic market.

DIFFERENCES IN STANDARDS

The differences in the standards are highly technical, but it is possible to summarize some of the key issues. In the presentation area, the central question is how graphics will be coded. The standards use a generally accepted code for letters and numbers, but they differ widely on presentation of shapes, colors and position on the screen.

Four kinds of graphics have been developed. The simplest is called "alphamosaic": this approach divides the TV screen into small boxes and fills some of them in. The result is a rough-edged, blocky design—a mosaic. This system produces inelegant graphics, but it is simple and requires relatively unsophisticated terminals.

The next level involves transmitting complex designs, such as advertisers' logos, to the terminal's memory. Short codes can be transmitted to call up these designs and tell the terminal how to use them. Two terms have been coined for variations of this technique: "Dynamically Redefinable Character Sets" (DRCS) and "Macros."

The third level is called "alphageometric." A set of geometric shapes (lines, arcs, circles and so on) is wired into the terminal, and the codes tell the terminal how to use them. This system produces sharp, detailed graphics, but it requires terminals with more built-in memory than those used for mosaics.

Finally, system designers are experimenting with "alphaphotographic" signals that produce still photographs in black and white or color. This level produces the best pictures, but it currently requires too much data transmission to be practical for narrowband services. Improvements in transmission efficiency (called "bandwidth compression") are likely to make alphaphotographic coding practical sometime in the future.

Presentation Issues

The North American presentation standard is based on a marketing judgment that advertisers and retailers will demand high quality graphics. It therefore has all the features except alphaphotographic, and it has a wide range of colors and advanced design features that give page creators maximum flexibility. To do all this, North American Standard terminals must be relatively elaborate and, when ordered in small quantities, relatively expensive.

As a result, some U.S. broadcasters are developing teletext systems that use only alphamosaics and DRCS. This requires less sophisticated gear, but it may lead to sale of a generation of terminals that is not compatible with the full North American Standard data bases that will appear on videotext. Broadcaster preference for the British system and cheap versions of the North American system apparently stems from a concern that consumers and advertisers will not pay as much for the small data bases on VBI teletext as they will for the much larger full channel and videotext services.

The Europeans also are more concerned with cost than with features. The British system that is being marketed in the United States provides only mosaics. Similarly, the CEPT Standard relies on mosaics, although DRCS and perhaps other features will be added.

The debate about the presentation level involves several other important issues:

Display Grid

The CEPT system is designed for a grid of 24 rows by 40 columns. The North American system is designed for U.S. television sets that have less resolution than the European sets, so it uses 20 rows by 40 columns, although it can accommodate other formats.

Error Resistance

Transmission errors are particularly likely in broadcast teletext because of interference from other over-the-air signals. There is considerable debate over which coding systems are most resistant to such errors and best able to identify and correct them. Test data thus far is inconclusive.

Efficiency

The number of pages that can be transmitted is crucial to system operators, particularly for services with small data bases and slow response times, i.e., narrowband teletext and telephone videotext. Efficiency depends on the number of bits that must be transmitted for each page, and that depends on the choice of standard and the complexity of the designs on the page. The North American standard transmits data only for the information to be displayed—it skips the blank spaces—so it is more efficient than the British system for most pages.

Transmission Issues

As noted earlier, another package of standards issues involves transmission. This area is independent of the presentation level; any transmission system can work for any coding scheme. There are three key transmission issues: data rate, spectrum authorization and pulse characteristics.

Data Rate

Everyone agrees the data transmission rate should be as fast as possible, to maximize the number of pages in the system, so long as it does not create interference or excessive errors. CBS has proposed a rate of 5.72 megabytes/second (Mb/s) for broadcast teletext. The cable industry has expressed concern that this rate may be too high for old systems to handle. The FCC has not decided whether to standardize this area or let each broadcaster establish an individual rate. The issue, again, is compatibility—a terminal built for one data rate cannot receive others without costly modifications.

Spectrum Authorization

The FCC proposed immediate authorization of VBI lines 14, 15, 16, 17, 18, 20 and 21 for teletext. Teletext use on lines 10 through 13 causes interference on old television sets, so the Commission proposed that use of those lines be phased in during the period 1988–1991, when the gradual turnover of sets will have removed most of the old ones from use. Closed captioning for the hearing impaired would be allowed to continue on line 21; broadcasters would choose which service to provide. Broadcasters would not be required to use all the VBI lines that are to be allowed, but by doing so they could make VBI teletext a more substantial service than most system developers have recognized. A VBI service using all 11 lines could carry over 500 pages.

Pulse Shape and Strength

The main remaining issue in the FCC's rulemaking is how to regulate the size and strength of the digital signals to avoid interference to the regular video signal.

ONE STANDARD OR MANY?

Since the FCC has not taken an active role in establishing standards, interested U.S. companies are still deciding whether to agree on the

North American Standard or use varying systems. There are three reasons for the industry to settle on a single standard.

First, such an agreement would speed the growth of electronic publishing. Without a standard, consumers, manufacturers, broadcasters and others may hesitate to invest in equipment for fear that they will choose the wrong technology and lose their investment. Once a standard is set, mass production can begin, and such production, with its lower prices, is essential to building a mass market. Experience with manufacturing microprocessors shows that even terminals built to the sophisticated North American Standard will become easily affordable once they are built in quantity. Mass production should cut the cost of the microprocessor chips needed for the North American Standard to less than $20 per terminal and bring the differential in retail terminal price for a given level of resolution to about $10.[2]

Second, a standard will ensure compatibility. Without compatibility, consumers would have to buy several different terminals to participate in all the teletext and videotext services. The public's enthusiasm for electronic publishing is not that high, and the spread of incompatible gear would fragment the market. This would shrink the potential audience for each electronic publisher, reduce publishers' incentives to enter the business and hurt both the quantity and the quality of electronic publications.

Finally, if the United States settles on a standard quickly, U.S. companies will have a chance to compete for the world market with manufacturers and data base providers operating under the CEPT Standard.

It must be recognized that there is danger in setting a standard. If the decision is made too early, it can freeze out desirable advances in technology. For example, the FCC standard for regular television provides a lower resolution picture than the European standard because the Europeans waited longer to make their decision. Similarly, when the FCC picked a system for color television in the early 1950s, it had to change its mind after three years because the first choice did not work well.

In the case of electronic publishing, however, we have the benefit of a decade of experiments. This business is ready to move into the mass market, and equipment manufacturers must decide what to build. Delay and uncertainty in setting standards will slow those decisions and hobble the whole industry.

The FCC's choice of neutrality was unfortunate because the Commission could have set a presentation standard that would have provided certainty without sacrificing quality. On the other hand, an attempt to set a standard might have meant two years of delay for regulatory proceedings and court challenges. In any case, it is now up to the private sector leaders to settle on a standard and provide the certainty and compatibility this new business needs. The United States market clearly is rallying around the North American Standard for videotext, but teletext remains divided. Unless agreement comes quickly, consumers will need two terminals to receive all the broadcast teletext services in a city.

Meanwhile, the FCC can and should promptly complete its remaining task in launching broadcast teletext. It should authorize regular service on as many VBI lines as possible, and it should standardize the data rate and the signal characteristics so that manufacturers have as much certainty as possible.

FOOTNOTES

1. Notice of Proposed Rulemaking, B.C. Docket No. 81-741 (1981).
2. See filings in FCC Docket cited above.

9

Electronic Publishing and Privacy

Midway through George Orwell's *1984*, the hero meets an old man and asks him how "Big Brother" got started. The answer—things began to go wrong when someone invented two-way television.

By 1984, electronic publishing and home transaction services may well pose serious privacy problems. While no one is proposing to put cameras inside TV sets, these services will collect and transmit vast amounts of personal information. Existing privacy rules are woefully inadequate to protect that data.

The new systems raise two kinds of concerns. First, services that transmit personal information, such as electronic mail, raise the danger of interception—the same kind of problem as wiretapping. Second, videotext services that sell information by the page or provide transactions will collect massive, computerized files on subscribers' behavior— the same kind of information as bank or insurance records.

These dangers to privacy are not serious for teletext. Because one-way systems send identical signals to large numbers of people, they will not handle private information, except for the possibility of individually addressed electronic mail over teletext. These systems will create no personal records except a list of subscribers; while some may be concerned about those lists, the fact that one subscribes to teletext is not particularly sensitive information. Videotext is the major focus of concern because it may transmit personal data and because its operators are certain to collect personal records.

ELECTRONIC EAVESDROPPING

Privacy protection for places is rooted in the common law of trespass and the constitutional safeguard against unreasonable searches. Statutes and court decisions have extended this concept to provide strong safeguards for personal communications through the mails and the telephone network.

In the case of videotext, several kinds of interception are possible. A cable subscriber using special equipment may be able to listen on his cable and pick up signals coming from or intended for other subscribers. A determined eavesdropper may put a physical tap on a telephone line or may dial into the central computer that transmits messages and keeps records. Finally, law enforcement agents may put recording equipment into videotext switching centers or on the lines that carry videotext signals.

Current Laws

Two federal laws affect this kind of interception. Title III of the Omnibus Crime Control and Safe Streets Act of 1968[1] provides criminal sanctions against unauthorized interception of wire communications and regulates wiretapping by law enforcement authorities. This law says that the government can wiretap only with a court order—which judges are to grant sparingly—or, in the case of national security investigations, on an order from the Attorney General. The other statute is Section 605 of the Communications Act,[2] which prohibits unauthorized interception of some signals.

Unfortunately, these laws were written during a simpler era in communications technology, and they leave wide loopholes in protection of data transmission. Title III defines "intercept" as the "aural acquisition of the contents of any wire or oral communication," and the word "aural" probably does not cover textual messages. While there has been no court case involving videotext, several appellate decisions have held that the law was written to protect telephone conversations and does not cover computer-to-computer transmissions because those are not "aural." Thus, Title III seems to provide no protection for videotext. Moreover, this law defines "wire communication" as transmission provided by a common carrier. Cable television is not considered common carriage, so it seems to be excluded.

Section 605 does apply to messages and is not limited to common carriers. However, Congress intended Title III to define the safeguards for wire transmissions, so when it passed that Act it amended section 605 to limit most of its provisions to over-the-air services. If Section 605 now protects wire transmissions at all—the law is unclear—it applies only when a system operator intercepts a message from a system and divulges it. Even in that situation, Section 605 permits divulgence "on demand of . . . lawful authority"—language that may allow system operators to allow law enforcement agencies to listen in on request, without a court order.

These loopholes will present serious privacy threats when electronic mail and other personalized data services are in general use. Private investigators and criminals may try to pick up videotext signals. Law enforcement agencies probably will be as eager to tap into the financial transactions and electronic mail of suspected criminals as they have been to tap into telephone conversations. Such official eavesdropping should not be forbidden—it may prove a useful investigative tool—but it should be controlled. Apart from the risk of abuse from unrestricted eavesdropping, people may be reluctant to use the electronic systems until they are given a reasonable expectation that their transactions will be private. The solution is to make private wiretapping a criminal offense and require a court order for official eavesdropping.

If Congress considers such legislation it will debate whether to apply the strict standards of Title III or a weaker test for a court order. That decision is less important than the basic step of providing judicial oversight and a formal procedure. Regrettably, privacy is a low priority issue in Congress, so legislation is likely to wait until videotext eavesdropping produces some kind of scandal.

INFORMATION PRIVACY

While physical privacy concepts are deeply rooted in common law, privacy for personal information is a new and poorly established principle. The intellectual mainspring for this idea was a classic 1890 *Harvard Law Review* article, "The Right of Privacy," co-authored by future Supreme Court Justice Louis Brandeis. The authors were concerned about publication of personal information in a newspaper—not the kind of physical invasion that trespass concepts cover. They argued that "recent inventions," such as photography, newspapers and others, jeopardized what they called "the right to be left alone." In the succeeding 90 years the courts have struggled with this idea, and some of the principles they have developed, such as a person's right to control use of his picture in advertising, will apply to videotext.

The focus of current debate, however, and the key issue for videotext, is the collection and use of personal records. Some videotext operations will produce massive files on subscribers' behavior. If the operator bills by the page, as opposed to setting a uniform charge per minute of use, then his computer must keep a record of each page each subscriber calls up. If the system is used for transactions such as shopping or bill-paying from home, then the store or bank must keep a record, and the system operator may want to keep his own record as protection against claims of errors. Thus, videotext may produce extensive, computerized records of the information subscribers use, the things they buy, the money they spend, and the times at which they do all these things. When these pieces of data are put together, they may provide detailed profiles of individual activities and interests.

While some of this information already is collected, e.g., by banks, videotext will collect new types of records and will put hitherto separate files into the same computer. The problem is magnified in the case of cable TV by "pay by the view" television that may generate records of the X-rated movies one watches, as well as burglar alarm systems that may record one's movements around the house. In the future, two-way systems may be used to turn on lights, heaters and appliances by computer command, creating even more records.

Videotext operators might be tempted to sell this data to direct mailers, retailers, pollsters or credit investigators. Much of it may be useful to law enforcement agencies as well. The commercial value of these records is indicated by the active market in magazine subscription lists; videotext records should provide much more detailed and useful mailing lists. Finally, these records might get into the wrong hands; one can easily imagine disclosure of politicians' private viewing habits or electronic robbery by manipulating computer records.

Videotext records raise information privacy dangers to a new dimension. This may present a major marketing and public relations problem for videotext operators, but the legal issues are not new. Government agencies, doctors, banks and insurance companies have long maintained sensitive personal files, many of them kept in computers. A debate over privacy rules for those records has been underway for a decade, and the conclusions apply equally to videotext.

The starting point is with the Supreme Court decision that individuals have no inherent legal interest in records that concern themselves but which are owned by others. In the key decision the Court said that a bank customer had no standing to contest his bank's disclosure of records concerning him to law enforcement authorities.[3] The same rule applies to a videotext operator's subscriber records, unless legislation or contract gives the subscriber additional rights. Thus, system operators are legally free to sell files or allow government agents to examine them, all without notifying the subscriber.

The solution is a set of rules for handling this personal data. Most of the conceptual work to develop these rules was done five years ago by a federal Privacy Commission that studied the use and misuse of medical, bank and insurance records. Its report and subsequent work in the cable area suggest seven principles for videotext records:

Notice: Subscribers should be notified of a system's two-way capabilities and of any records the company intends to keep.

Consent: Written subscriber consent should be obtained for collection of any information from two-way systems, except for data recorded to maintain technical operations, monitor for billing, or detect unauthorized users. The consent form should indicate how the records will be used, including whether they will be disclosed, in individual or aggregate form, to third parties. Customers should be able to sign up for any service without having any individually identifiable information disclosed to third parties.

Right to See, Copy and Correct: Subscribers should be able to see and copy—at their own expense—any records concerning them. The company should be obliged to correct any errors.

Government Access: Records should be made available to government officials only in response to compulsory legal process. In general, the subscriber should be notified and given an opportunity to contest such access. Notice may be omitted if it would jeopardize an investigation, but the operator should insist on a court order in such cases.

Retention: Records should be destroyed when they are no longer needed.

Security: The company should be obliged to keep records secure.

Liability: The company should be liable for any damages resulting from misuse or unauthorized disclosure of records.

Except for notice, these duties should rest on the recordkeeper. Thus, if a cable system offers home banking and the bank keeps the only records of the transactions, then the bank, not the cable operator, should be responsible. In addition, the rules should not distinguish between cable and telephone-based systems.

The philosophy behind these principles is to let people know what is happening and give them the right to make their own decisions, *without* having the government decide what kinds of records should be collected or how they should be used. Therefore, this code does not forbid anything. Laws should not pre-judge technology—especially in this fast-moving field—or make assumptions about public attitudes. Some people may *want* their records disclosed; for example, when the association of direct mailers offered several years ago to remove any name from its members' list on request, more people wanted their names added than deleted. The key legal principle is that each subscriber should be told, in advance, how the records will be used. If people do care about privacy, this rule should prompt system operators at least to offer them the option of total protection.

These principles can be established for videotext through federal or state legislation or, for systems using cable TV, through requirements by local authorities as part of franchise agreements. Only one state (Illinois) has passed such a law; it forbids installation of monitoring devices or disclosure of lists of subscribers or viewing habits without subscriber consent. Many city councils are setting some privacy rules through the cable franchise process. A survey of 21 large cities that awarded franchises in 1979 and 1980 found that four-fifths of them established some privacy rules (they usually require individual knowledge and consent before any two-way service is installed), although few of them covered more than two of the principles listed above.

Voluntary Commitments

Many potential videotext operators are voluntarily pledging some degree of privacy protection. For example, AT&T has a policy against disclosure of customer records except in response to compulsory process. Warner-Amex, the cable company that operates the interactive "Qube" cable television system in Columbus, Ohio, announced a privacy code in December 1981. It says the central computer will record individual responses "only where necessary," gives subscribers the right to correct information, and says that records will be given to law enforcement agents only in response to a court order or grand jury subpoena. It does not, however, require specific consent to collect or disclose personal data.

To make such voluntary commitments legally binding and ensure that the customer has standing to go to court if these commitments are violated, they should be included in the videotext operator's contract with subscribers. Legal liability also would give the operator an incentive to design safeguards against mistaken disclosure or theft of personal records.

Public concern about information privacy for videotext is legitimate, and it may make people hesitant to use this technology. On the other hand, the privacy threats are only theoretical; few videotext records are being collected at present, and no cases of abuse have been reported so far. While experience with other kinds of records provides a basis to legislate the general principles outlined above, it is too early to decide what additional detailed requirements may be needed. Moreover, the proliferation of varying state and local privacy rules poses a serious threat to national services—varying rules could force system operators to maintain hundreds of separate records systems and treat each one differently.

The best answer is to develop an industry-wide privacy code. Where local authorities want to legislate, they should be urged to follow a uniform formula, as legislators often do in other areas of the law. If some in the industry do mishandle their records and Congress does decide to act, it will then have a tested model.

FOOTNOTES

1. 18 U.S.C. 2510-2520.
2. 47 U.S.C. 605.
3. *United States v. Miller*, 425 U.S. 435 (1976).
4. Privacy Act of 1974, 88 Stat. 1896.
5. *Community Television Review*, July, 1981.

10

Defamation and Obscenity*

All publishers must exercise care about the material they publish. Whether they are covered by the Communications Act or not, they may be liable under state and local laws covering two important kinds of content: defamation and obscenity. In both cases, the new technology raises questions about old rules written for print or broadcasting.

DEFAMATION

In general, electronic publishers may be sued for libel just like their print and broadcast brethren. However, the new medium raises complexities in determining who is liable and under what standard.

Electronic publishers compile their data bases in two ways: original composition and purchase of others' material. In the first case, the electronic publisher is in the same position as a print publisher. If the material libels[1] someone, the publisher can be sued for damages. However, the First Amendment limits this liability for the media, including electronic publishers. The rationale behind this First Amendment privilege is that society's interest in a free, uncensored press can outweigh an individual's interest in personal reputation.

In 1964, the Supreme Court ruled that otherwise defamatory comments or opinions published by the media about public officials are constitutionally protected unless the publication is made with "actual malice."[2] This term has been defined to mean "actual knowledge of falsity or reckless disregard for the truth." This is a difficult burden to meet, so it gives the media broad protection against defamation suits. The Court later extended this protection to media coverage of public figures.[3]

---

*This chapter was co-authored by Abbe Lowell of the Washington law firm of Venable, Baetjer, Howard & Civiletti.

For private individuals, however, the Court ruled that states could fashion their own rules "as long as they do not impose liability without fault."[4] States are permitted to decide that a private individual can sue a publisher and win if the publisher fails to exercise reasonable care in checking the accuracy of the information. Since this decision, nearly half the states have adopted this negligence standard, a handful have applied the "actual malice" test and the remainder have either not decided or have adopted a hybrid.

The Electronic Publisher's Role and Liability

Electronic publishing that carries news clearly falls under these First Amendment policies. However, some services will provide non-news items, such as airline schedules, classified advertisements and the like. This material is called "commercial speech." The Court has not yet decided whether the "actual malice" standard applies, and commercial speech may enjoy a reduced level of protection.[5]

Another liability issue involves the electronic publisher's actual role in preparing the material. Under current law, each individual who takes part in making a publication is called a "primary publisher" and can be sued for any defamatory statement in the publication.[6] Thus, defamation suits usually are brought against both the reporter and the newspaper. In addition, anyone who repeats the defamatory statement is a "republisher" and also can be held liable, even if he states his source and disclaims any assertion of accuracy. The law holds republishers responsible for what they publish, as though they had written it. Thus, if a newspaper runs a defamatory wire service story, the vast majority of jurisdictions will hold the newspaper liable, even if the source is identified and the content is not changed.[7]

The law does, however, protect some in the publishing chain. Those who simply "deliver" the material, e.g., newspaper vendors and video tape technicians, are known as "secondary publishers." These people can be held liable only if they have actual knowledge that the material is defamatory.[8]

Newspaper vendors often are not wealthy enough for plaintiffs to bother arguing whether they ought to be liable, but the issue will have great importance for teletext and videotext system operators—often large corporations—that take their material from others. The determination of whether an electronic publisher may be liable is likely to depend on the type and scope of any editing and on how the electronic publisher describes the source of the data. For example, a cable system may lease a channel to a newspaper, signing a contract that abjures all content control. Unlike the relationship of a wire service to a newspaper, the cable operator in this case neither makes editorial judgments nor puts its name behind the content. Therefore, the operator probably would be treated as a secondary publisher.

The situation is more complex if the electronic publisher can change the format, e.g., to fit the demands of the medium, but not the content. A reasonable policy is to treat electronic publishers as secondary publishers if they merely take others' material, electronically "cut and paste" it for insertion in the data base and identify the source. Such an operator should be liable only for its *own* mistakes—e.g., if a fact were accidentally changed.

However, if the operator exercises more control, e.g., by choosing the articles to put in the data base, and editing the content, or if it fails to disclose the source of the information, then a court probably would rule that the operator had taken responsibility for the content. The electronic publisher would become a republisher and could be sued.[9] One precedent for this approach is the FCC's policy of applying the broadcasting content rules to cable channels which the operator controls but not to "access channels" controlled by others. A precedent with a much longer history is the policy governing common carriers such as telegraph and telephone companies. These entities provide access to all and exercise no content control. In general, they are liable only for their own errors, and even then their tariffs often limit liability to the price the sender paid to have the message sent. This approach has been held to be a desirable policy, because it makes common carriage—i.e., nondiscriminatory access for all—practical. If the carrier were responsible for content, it would have read the messages and reserved the rights to reject some.

For the same reason, electronic publishers should be allowed to avoid liability if they operate as carriers, i.e., by renting space in data bases to any information provider who wants to use it, without controlling the content. The Communications Act may make this arrangement impossible for radio and television broadcasting because it makes the licensees fully responsible for the content on their channels. However, common carrier treatment should be available for electronic publishing on MDS, cable leased channels, and telephone-based services. In addition, if the courts uphold the FCC's proposal to treat the FM SCA and TV VBI as "hybrids," then carrier status may be available for them also.

"Single Publication" Rule

Another complication raised by defamation on teletext or videotext is the so-called "single publication" rule. This rule says that an entire edition of a newspaper, magazine, book or other publication is treated as one publication, which occurs when the finished product is released for sale.[10] States have time limits (called "statutes of limitation") on suits for defamation, and this rule sets the starting date. For example, if a book is first distributed on January 1, 1982, and the statute of limitations for libel is one year, then a suit would have to be brought by January 1, 1983, regardless of when the person defamed may have bought the book.

If a videotext system merely reproduces pages from a newspaper, for example, then the time period clearly begins when the newspaper is published. The situation is more complicated, however, for a data base that originates its own material and constantly updates it. Such a system does not have "editions," so some other benchmark must be developed. The most likely tests are the time a given page is put into the data base and the time it is first retrieved. Of course, some systems will not have records of when the data was first inserted or used or, for that matter, whether anyone saw it.

A related issue is the extent of damages. Despite the "single publication" rule, damages for defamation are measured by the overall effect of the item on readers during the entire period the item has been in circulation.[11] The advent of electronic publishing raises the risk. For example, videotext can take an item published in a magazine with a circulation of a few thousand and make it available to millions. When courts assess damages, they must decide whether this potential exposure requires a higher damage figure.

Keeping Records

Finally, electronic publishers must consider the need to keep records. To defend against defamation actions, publishers often need to prove what was said, when and in what context—i.e., whether the item was expressed as fact or opinion. Many electronic publishing services can work without any paper or other permanent records, but wise operators will maintain complete recordings, e.g., on computer tape.

OBSCENITY

Teletext and videotext can provide impressive graphics, but using them for erotic pictures would require an extraordinary imagination. On the other hand, the kinds of "personal classifieds" that some newspapers carry are bound to turn up in data bases. Promoters of obscene books and movies may use electronic publishing to advertise. Moreover, in a few more years we will have photographs on these systems. Already, the videotext company called "The Source" has found some racy messages on the electronic "bulletin board" it operates, and the British videotext service has had to deal with a computer "Guide to Dirty Books." Thus disputes over obscenity are inevitable, and they will pose two key questions: who is liable and under what standard.

The first issue is conceptually the same as for defamation. A system operator that creates or controls the content should be liable for it. One that just manages a system and has no content role should not be liable, just as a telephone company cannot be prosecuted for a subscriber's obscene phone calls.

Unfortunately, politics may complicate this policy. State courts are likely to make the decisions on defamation, but legislatures can be expected to step in to police obscenity themselves. Already, cablecasting of "adult films" has prompted Utah to pass and other states to consider restrictive legislation.[12] Some of these laws will impinge on expressions protected by the First Amendment, and most probably will fail to distinguish between video and electronic publishing or between content creation and data base management. Overreaching politicians intent on halting obscenity may write laws to hold all system operators responsible for content; after all, an operator with a heavy investment may be more cautious about brushes with the law than people who make pornographic films. Unfortunately, this kind of broad legislation would force operators to review content and reserve the right to reject material. That, in turn, would increase the operator's risk of liability for defamation as well as obscenity. Caution would prompt operators to reject material that the First Amendment protects. True "carrier" data bases would be impossible. The society would lose some of the diversity of ideas and authors that the technology makes possible. Those who write obscenity rules should exercise restraint and give pure carriers a chance.

Supreme Court's Obscenity Standard

The other issue is how far government can go in regulating obscenity on electronic publishing before it violates the First Amendment. By way of background, the Supreme Court has set out a three-point standard for determining what is obscene:[13]

> a) whether the average person, applying contemporary standards would find that the work, taken as a whole, appeals to the prurient interest. . . .;
> b) whether the work depicts or describes in a patently offensive way sexual conduct specifically defined by the applicable state law; and
> c) whether the work, taken as a whole, lacks serious literary, artistic, political or scientific value.

State and local obscenity laws governing the print media and films must be consistent with these principles and must be reasonably precise. Broad bans on indecent material can deter publication of material protected by the First Amendment, so the federal courts have developed a policy of striking down "vague" laws.

In the case of broadcasting, however, the Supreme Court has upheld the Communications Act's prohibition on airing "obscene, indecent or profane language."[14] In *FCC v. Pacifica Foundation,* the Court held that the "pervasive" character of broadcasting justifies regulation that would be unconstitutional for print.[15] This case began when a father and his son were listening to their car radio during the middle of the day and heard a portion of a monologue by comedian George Carlin about the words that could not be used on the air. The station had provided a warning at the beginning of the program that the material might be offensive, but the father and son had not heard it. Following the father's complaint, the FCC disciplined the station and adopted a policy statement barring stations from broadcasting "language that described in terms patently offensive as measured by contemporary community standards for the broadcast medium, sexual or excretory activities and organs, at times of the day when there is a reasonable risk that children may be in the audience."[16] The Supreme Court bought the FCC's argument that "[t]he passive act of listening to the radio is different, practically, socially, and physically, from obtaining literature or gaining admission to a movie theater."[17] An implicit part of this conclusion is that parents may have more control over the books and movies their children use than over the radio and television.

The Court's vote was five-to-four and its opinion was written narrowly, focusing on the specific facts of the case. Nevertheless, the principle has been established, so the question for electronic publishing is whether it is more closely related to the "deliberate act" of purchasing and reading a book or attending a movie or the passive reception of broadcasting, which "comes directly into the home and frequently without advance warning of its content."[18] As usual, the problem is that the new technology falls athwart the dividing line between print and broadcasting.

Print vs. Broadcasting Rules

Vague rules against "indecency" would limit services consumers may want and cause stifling uncertainty and self-censorship, so the right answer is the print model. Fortunately, this is also the likely answer. It seems certain for subscription services, because the user must act to sign up for the service and then take several more actions to enter the data base and call up individual pages. Advertiser-supported teletext is a closer call because it is broadcast over-the-air and available to all. Even in that case, however, most teletext services will require the viewer to act—i.e., push a button—to display a page. If the index that lists the pages in the system provides notice of the "indecent" pages, then this service certainly involves the kind of user consent that calls for print-type treatment. The First Amendment should prevent the FCC or any other governmental body from acting against "indecent" content on such a system. If parents wish to keep their children from watching some items, they should use locks or codes that limit access, rather than rely on outside censorship.

Application of print-type rules does not mean that all is clear. For example, the Supreme Court of Nevada recently upheld a state law that banned advertising by brothels in certain areas.[19] The Court ruled that such advertising was "commercial speech" not protected by the First Amendment. The constitutional standard on obscenity is vague on this and other points, and it is constantly being reinterpreted. The best electronic publishers can hope for is that they will be treated the same as print publishers, not singled out for special treatment.

FOOTNOTES

1. There are two categories of defamation: libel (written) and slander (oral). Broadcasting, i.e., the spoken publication of a written news text, has broken down some of the distinction between libel and slander. *See Restatement (Second) of Torts*, § 586A (1977). In addition, the distinction is far less important when First Amendment-protected media are involved.

2. *New York Times v. Sullivan*, 376 U.S. 254 (1964). Before *New York Times*, the media, like anyone else, could be found liable if a person proved the falsity of a statement and damages. *Peck v. Tribune Co.*, 214 U.S. 185 (1909). Fault or intent was not a factor.

3. *Curtis Publishing Co. v. Butts*, 388 U.S. 130 (1967).

4. *Gertz v. Robert Welch, Inc.*, 418 U.S. 323 (1974). Defamation litigation often revolves around arguments over whether the plaintiff is a private individual or a public figure. *See, e.g., Hutchinsome v. Proxmire*, 433 U.S. 111 (1979) (Supreme Court ruled that a research scientist receiving Federal funds and named as winner of Senator Proxmire's "Golden Fleece" award was *not* a public figure).

5. The Supreme Court has suggested different treatment for commercial and noncommercial speech. *Virginia State Board of Pharmacy v. Virginia Citizens Consumer Council, Inc.*, 425 U.S. 748, 771 n.24 (1976). Other courts have ruled that the same standards should apply. *See e.g., Bose Corp. v. Consumers Union of United States, Inc.*, 508 F. Supp. 249 (D. Mass. 1981).

6. Prosser, *Law of Torts*, § 113, p. 768-769 (4th ed. 1971).

7. *Restatement (Second) of Torts*, § 578; Prosser, *Law of Torts*, § 113, p. 775.

8. *Restatement (Second) of Torts*, § 581, states that "one who only delivers or transmits defamatory matter published by a third person is subject to liability if, but only if, he knows or has reason to know of its defamatory character."

9. *See Restatement (Second) of Torts*, § 581, Comment on Section (2) (broadcasters treated as republishers because they "initiate, select and put upon the air their own programs" or "permit others to use their facilities").

10. *Restatement (Second) of Torts*, § 577A(3).

11. *Restatement (Second) of Torts*, § 577A(4).

12. *Home Box Office, Inc. v. Wilkenson*, 531 F. Supp., p. 987 (D.C. Utah 1982).

13. *Miller v. California*, 413 U.S. 1524 (1973).

14. 18 U.S.C. § 1464.

15. *FCC v. Pacifica Foundation*, 438 U.S. 726 (1978).

16. *Pacifica Foundation*, 56 F.C.C.2d 94 (1975).

17. *FCC's Brief in Pacifica Foundation v. FCC* at 13.

18. *In re WHUY-FM Eastern Educational Radio*, 24 F.C.C.2d 408, (1970).

19. *Princess Sea Industries, Inc. v. Nevada*, 635 P.2d (Nev. 1981).

11

Economic Rights: Copyright, Piracy and Retransmission

Information is a product with a value. Electronic publishers will need to acquire it and protect their rights to it. Here again, the new technology raises questions for policies that were framed with print and video in mind.

COPYRIGHT

The first problem for the electronic publisher is obtaining the right to disseminate the information. Some of the data base content will be created by the publishers' employees, and work done for hire belongs to the employer. However, journalists' unions are showing increasing interest in negotiating separate payment for electronic publication, e.g., when articles written for print are reproduced on videotext.

Publishers also buy distribution rights from authors and other publishers. Until recently, publishers generally assumed that print publication rights included electronic distribution, but that is changing. Information providers, such as wire services, are beginning to sell print and electronic rights as separate products requiring separate payments. This involves no regulatory issues; the rights are determined by the individual contracts, and the new medium simply is spawning a new set of contracts.

More complex issues arise when publishers try to control the use of their material. Some electronic publishers will be making major investments to obtain information and design electronic pages, and they expect to make money by selling the data for substantial per-minute or per-page charges. These businesses will depend upon protection against unauthorized copying and resale.

Copyright Act Provisions

In this area, rights are established by the Copyright Act, which protects "works of authorship" against infringement.[1] Copyright protection attaches from the moment a work is "fixed in any tangible medium of expression" from which it can be "perceived, reproduced, or otherwise communicated, either directly or with the aid of a machine or device."

Other statements in the law and legislative history make it clear that computer data bases may be copyrighted. Individual entries may be protected, as may the overall data base to the extent that the compilation is itself a "work."[2] However, creation of an electronic frame that exists only momentarily is not sufficient. The material must be "fixed,"—i.e., recorded on some storage system, such as paper or a computer disc—before, or simultaneously with, the transmission. Once made, such records need not be retained, although sensible publishers will do so to deal with any disputes about content, as well as to reinforce the copyright.

Unauthorized reproduction on paper or in another computer memory is an infringement, as is unauthorized retransmission. The reproduction occurs when the material is put into or taken out of a computer memory. The right to sue does not require proof that the copied data base has been used. Infringement can give the publisher the right to sue for an injunction or to recover damages.

The material should carry a notice of the copyright claim, the name of the author, and the year of publication. The notice must be sufficiently conspicuous to make people aware of the claim. Regulations recently promulgated by the Copyright Office indicate that for electronic publishing the notice may be placed on the first frame the user sees when access to the data base begins. Notice need not appear on each frame.

A publisher can sue only after the item has been "registered" and copies filed with the Library of Congress. Data bases that are not published in hard copy form need not be filed, but the Copyright Office is asking that representative frames—e.g., the index—be filed. It is not yet clear whether copies must be on paper or whether computer discs will do. There is no need to register at the time of publication, but a publisher who does not register within three months may not recover automatic damages or attorney's fees. In such a case, the publisher is limited to injunctive relief and the actual damages the infringement caused, but actual damages are often difficult to prove.

"Fair Use"

The electronic publisher does face some complications in the copyright field. First, the Copyright Act lets recipients of copyrighted material make "fair use" of it. This provision allows copying and reuse of the material without the publishers' permission if the use is limited to a small and insubstantial portion of the work and does not adversely affect its commercial value. The idea is to allow private users to copy a few pages for non-commercial use, and the Act gives extra leeway to schools, libraries and other nonprofit groups.

The "fair use" concept is notoriously imprecise, and it may create even more uncertainty for electronic publications than for print documents. For example, the provision may permit a videotext subscriber to record portions of a data base on a home computer and retrieve individual pages later, as long as the data is not to be sold to others. However, in a comparable situation, a federal appeals court has held that home video taping of television shows is infringement. If the Supreme Court agrees, the likely result will be to place a surcharge on sales of video tape recorders and distribute that money to copyright holders. Thus, it is impossible to predict what will happen if home recording of videotext pages becomes popular.

Publication

Second, the Act defines the concept of "publication" in a way that will exclude many teletext and videotext services. Merely making a data base available to users by display is not "publication"; that status applies only if the intention is that the data will be reproduced—in print or electronic form—by subscribers or middlemen. An "unpublished" data base has copyright protection even if it has no copyright notice and has not been registered, although electronic publishers would be wise to use the notice. In any case, the fact that a videotext service may be used by millions of people throughout the country but is not considered "published'" shows the extent to which technology has outstripped the law.

Eligibility

The third problem is that much material is not eligible for copyright. The protection covers the author's intellectual property—the manner in which something is expressed or communicated—but not facts or ideas. For example, the way election results are presented may be copyrightable, but the results themselves are not.

This dividing line is fuzzy, and the new technology will produce uncertainty and disputes. For example, *The New York Times* operates a videotext service that abstracts news reported in private newsletters. Electronic transmission gets the information to the newsletter subscribers before the newsletters themselves arrive in the mail. The newsletter publishers have complained about infringement, while *The Times* has taken the position that it is simply distributing facts. *The Times* gave up in this case, but similar disputes will be a regular theme of electronic publishing.

A second example: airline schedules are in the public domain, so that an entrepreneur might subscribe to a videotext service that includes these schedules, store them electronically in a data base and resell that data base. The original publisher can be protected only by ensuring that each frame has a special design or other copyrightable characteristic.

Protection and Enforcement

Electronic publishers have some options to increase their protection. For example, reproduction and reuse may be expressly limited in the contract between the publisher and the subscribers. Such a provision would give a publisher the right to sue for breach of contract, as well as for copyright violation, should infringement occur.

Finally, copyright is hard to enforce. The new technology makes it easy for a teletext or videotext subscriber to transfer copyrighted material from the publisher's data base to his own. It is difficult for the system operator to detect such infringements, and litigation to halt them and recover damages is slow and costly. This problem is not new, of course; paper copiers are constantly used to infringe copyrights.

As a practical matter, some electronic publishers will not have to worry about these problems. If the information in the data base has low resale value or high time sensitivity, there is little incentive to copy and reuse it. However, some electronic publishing pages will be expensive to create and easy to copy and retransmit. Electronic publishers who plan on operating such systems must anticipate some copyright problems.

SIGNAL INTERCEPTION

A second problem involves interception of copyrighted material. In this case, the problem is not copying and resale; rather, it is that people may steal services instead of paying for them. Such "piracy" has been a thorn in the side of pay television operators, and it may trouble those who provide expensive, subscription electronic publishing services, especially over-the-air.

The legal issue here is whether interception is lawful, since some argue the airwaves belong to everyone. In the last two years, a series of court cases seems to have settled that question in favor of the publishers. Section 605 of the Communications Act has been held to bar the sale or use of decoders to intercept signals intended for subscribers. Violation is a basis for criminal prosecution or private civil action.[3]

Legal rights, however, do not solve the problem. A teletext operator has no way to detect interception by unauthorized decoders. Even videotext is vulnerable to persons who determine how to dial into data bases without paying for them. If interception is discovered, it is difficult to turn off the service. Legal action can be taken against companies that manufacture "bootleg" decoders, but it is not practical to find or prosecute all the individuals who may try to steal electronic publishing information. Thus, electronic publishers who sell extremely valuable information must consider expensive encryption or other technological defenses against information piracy.

CABLE RETRANSMISSION OF TELETEXT

The Copyright Act has a special provision to permit cable TV operators to retransmit over-the-air TV signals without the broadcaster's permission. This "compulsory license" raises a special copyright issue for vertical blanking interval (VBI) teletext. This provision gives cable operators the right to retransmit VBI teletext services intended for the general public, although it does not appear to cover encoded, subscriber-supported services.

The broadcaster and the program creator are supposed to be reimbursed for the use of their signal by payments from a royalty pool collected from cable operators. The division of these royalties is determined by the Copyright Royalty Tribunal and currently is the subject of considerable controversy, together with the size of the fees and the adequacy of the entire system. If broadcast teletext is retransmitted on cable, information providers such as newspapers may join the crowd of broadcasters, movie producers and others who are fighting over this pool of money.

Deleting Teletext Signal

There is also a legal dispute when the cable operator wants to retransmit the broadcaster's television program but drop the accompanying teletext signal. This is the situation in the first law suit involving VBI teletext, *WGN Broadcasting Co. v. United Video, Inc.*[4] WGN is a television station that is conducting a VBI teletext experiment. United Video is a satellite carrier that picks up WGN's television signal and relays it to cable systems. United Video is developing its own teletext service for cable, so when it reconstitutes the signal for transmission to the satellite it removes WGN's teletext and substitutes its own.

United Video relays WGN's programs under the compulsory license provision. The Act says this permission applies only if the carrier exercises no "control over the content,"[5] and the cable operator does not "alter the content of the particular program . . . or [alter or delete] any commercial advertising or station announcements transmitted . . . during or immediately before or after [it]."

WGN sued for copyright infringement, arguing that the VBI teletext service is integral to the regular broadcast, so United Video cannot use one without the other. United Video responded that teletext is a separate service, so the carrier and cable operator are free to retransmit it or delete it, regardless of what they do with the television programs.

The judge agreed with United Video, and the decision makes sense although it is on appeal. The Copyright Act's purpose is to protect creative works, so the policy should depend on the nature of the programming. Teletext normally has its own content, independent of the television shows that appear on regular television channels. A typical VBI teletext service such as WGN's runs the same set of pages throughout the day, without changing content as the station moves from one television program to another.

The Copyright Act forbids deletion of the advertising that is broadcast with each television program, in order to protect the station's economic interest, but it does not require a cable operator can retransmit some programs and not others. Similarly, the cable system should be able to retransmit television and not teletext. The two should be considered separate, copyrightable works. If this approach is followed, cable systems will make a separate royalty payment for teletext retransmissions, and the Copyright Royalty Tribunal will set up a special formula to distribute that money.

This policy runs into problems if the teletext service has pages directly related to the simultaneous television program. The *WGN* decision said that in such cases teletext and regular programs might turn out to be a single "work" for copyright purposes. Examples of this kind of teletext include "closed captioning" of television programs for the hearing-impaired and television advertisements that urge viewers to switch to the advertiser's teletext page. The latter situation is particularly difficult because of the statutory requirement quoted above that advertisements transmitted with the television program be left intact.

On the other hand, special talent and equipment are needed to create teletext pages. The job of creating them is a separate "work of authorship" from the creation of television programs. Moreover if the copyright status of each teletext service were to depend on the proportion of its pages that relate to simultaneous television programs, the result would be confusion and litigation. Therefore, the best policy is to treat all teletext services as separate from regular programs for copyright purposes.

FOOTNOTES

1. 17 U.S.C. § 102(a).
2. 17 U.S.C. § 103(a); H.R. Rep. No. 1476, 94th Cong., 2d Sess. 57 (1976).
3. See cases cited in Chapter 5, footnote 9.
4. *WGN Continental Broadcasting Co. v. United Video, Inc.*, 523 F. Supp. 403 (N.D. Ill. 1981).
5. 17 U.S.C. 111(a) (3).

12

Conclusion

Electronic publishing has tremendous advantages. It gives publishers a way to avoid the surging costs of paper, printing and physical delivery. It offers rapid, convenient access—from the home or office—to virtually unlimited amounts of information. Teletext and videotext may become a primary information medium by the end of this century. If so, the policy decisions discussed in this book will be as important as those made a half century ago that shaped the birth of broadcasting.

On the other hand, the development of electronic publishing will take a decade or more, and it may not get far at all. The success of this medium depends not only on the creativity of its promoters but on the public's willingness to use video screens instead of paper. Many people may decline that trade.

Policymakers cannot predict what will happen and should not try to base their decisions on guesses about the future. Rather, the policies for this new medium should reflect the principles the United States adopted for print two centuries ago: freedom for publishers and diversity for audiences.

NEED FOR DEREGULATION

The first theme translates into a deregulation policy. Government should give this new medium as much freedom as possible, so that all its possible applications will have a chance to be tested. As a general principle, electronic publishers should be treated the same way as their colleagues in print. The specific actions that are needed include:

1. The Communications Act content rules, which were designed for broadcasting, should not be extended to electronic publishing. Because this medium offers diversity of voices and user control over the

127

information received, those rules are not needed, and applying them could stifle some voices.

The FCC should seek to classify broadcast teletext as a "hybrid" and to drop its rules for videotext over cable. At the same time, the Commission should clarify that its withdrawal does not open the field to state and local content regulation; it should preempt such controls except for obscenity and defamation. In those cases, electronic publishers should have as much leeway as their print brethren. In some areas, the FCC may lack the authority to deregulate, and Congress should act.

2. The FCC should free system operators to make any kinds of business arrangements they wish. Broadcasters should be free to provide advertiser-supported or subscription services and to provide "addressed" services, so they can use teletext for electronic mail. They should be allowed to originate content themselves or rely entirely on other information providers. Cable operators should be freed to carry or delete broadcasters' VBI teletext signals.

3. There should be no rate regulation for information services. Such regulation already exists for dial-up information provided by telephone companies; extending it to videotext could impose needless delays and costs on carriers' services at a time when others will be providing identical services without regulation. The FCC seems inclined to preempt such state or local controls, but its authority is so tangled that legislation may be necessary.

Rate regulation of transmission—as opposed to information—involves many services other than electronic publishing, so this medium's needs will not determine policy in that area. However, electronic publishers will be seriously affected by the rates for various transmission services and by the possible deregulation of data networks. Companies with a large stake in this new business should be involved in those debates.

Exceptions to Deregulation

This emphasis on deregulation should not be absolute, however. The new technology poses problems for some important social values, and each policy area must be examined on its own merits. A few regulations emerge as candidates for retention or even strengthening:

1. There is a case for retaining two of the broadcast content rules: the Equal Time requirement for paid advertising and the requirement to identify sponsored material. The first rule protects the political process,

and the second avoids deceiving readers; neither of them imposes any true burden.

2. Imposition of a mandatory technical standard would impinge on electronic publishers' freedom to experiment, but some consensus on a standard is needed to encourage production and purchase of terminals.

3. The new technology has opened loopholes in the laws against eavesdropping on private communications. Congress should act to preserve the principle that people have a right to privacy when they use electronic transmission for personal communications.

4. Videotext raises another kind of privacy danger from the creation and use of data banks full of personal information. System operators should adopt voluntary codes to prevent misuse of this information, while Congress and the states decide whether to legislate.

5. Copyright protection is essential to give electronic publishers the incentive to get into the business. The Copyright Act already has been amended to provide such protection for data bases, but care must be taken to keep the rules current with the technology.

Government Intervention to Promote Diversity

Finally, government intervention may be needed to promote diversity. This is most important, because electronic publishing has the potential for vigorous competition. It offers even the smallest information providers the chance to distribute their products and ideas to a national audience. Deregulation is premised on this diversity, but government intervention may be necessary to ensure that potential is realized. There are four specific points here:

1. The FCC should continue its open entry policy and its management of radio frequencies to maximize the number of electronic pipelines to the information consumer.

2. As long as the telephone network is the only way to reach the general public with videotext, there must be strict enforcement of carriers' obligation to provide transmission service to all, without discrimination. In addition, if those companies are allowed to originate their own videotext content, they will have the incentive and opportunity to reduce diversity by discriminating against competing publishers. Until there is competition in two-way transmission, it may be desirable to restrict carriers' electronic publishing activities if carriers do become electronic publishers—and at least the independent telephone companies are

certain to play that role—it is important to police their activities.

3. Cable television is the other potential bottleneck in the ability of information providers to transmit messages to homes. It is too soon to say whether cable will have enough advantage over telephone and over-the-air media to give it monopoly power, but it is appropriate to start debating and testing the idea of mandating leases of cable channels.

4. Bottlenecks that can stifle diversity may exist in the computers needed for electronic publishing, as well as in the transmission pipelines to the home. The danger that competition will be stifled seems more remote here, so mandatory access to data bases is neither necessary nor likely. However, policymakers should remove any barriers that discourage system operators from providing access to their data bases. Specifically, if an operator acts like a carrier, opens his data base to access by all information providers, and abjures control over the content, the legal system should free him of liability for the material. The Communications Act should be revised to make such operation possible for broadcasters, and state legislatures and courts should adopt appropriate obscenity and defamation rules.

NEW SOCIAL QUESTIONS

This book has focused on the rules that will tell electronic publishers what they can and cannot do. However, the new technology poses even more fundamental social questions that will demand answers in this decade. For example:

- What role should the government play in creating data bases and in making them available to the public? Project Green Thumb is a government-funded venture into videotext; should it be the first or the last?

- Teletext and videotext may affect union jurisdictions. Will the creation of electronic pages be handled by journalists, printers, broadcast technicians or some new labor category?

- As electronic publishing spreads, increasing amounts of information will be distributed electronically and will be difficult or impossible to obtain in print. Libraries may be able to provide such information only by violating their tradition of free access to all; they may have to charge users. If that happens, some people may find themselves unable to afford information they now get for free.

- No one thinks that newspapers are about to disappear, but electronic publishing and related applications do threaten our paper-based institutions. As mail is diverted to electronic transmission, the U.S. Postal Service will have increasing difficulty meeting its expenses. As postal rates go up and advertising revenue is siphoned away, some newspapers and magazines will feel the pinch. Electronic publishing poses a threat to diversity as well as an opportunity.

- The new technology may require skills as well as money. Teletext and videotext are being designed for the mass audience, but people who have no experience with computers may find it hard to get accustomed to these devices. The spread of more sophisticated computer applications through offices and factories poses major problems for children whose schools omit computer training. Moreover, the technology threatens to eliminate millions of low-skill jobs. Electronic mail, newspapers, banking and shopping will reduce the need for mailmen, delivery boys, bank tellers and retail clerks. The economy may become more efficient, but millions of people may find themselves excluded from it.

- Videotext may change our politics. Already a two-way cable system in Columbus, Ohio, is testing "instant polls." As videotext spreads, so will the capability to have millions of people "vote" on policy issues. Such polls may have no legal effect, but they are certain to influence politicians.

All these issues merit more attention than they are getting, and those who undertake this labor will need both imagination and modesty. The birth of electronic publishing is quite similar to the birth of printing. Some may have foreseen a downturn in the calligraphy industry, but few could have anticipated the tremendous impact on the medieval church, the economy and the political system.

We must now try to imagine all the new medium's possibilities, but we must also recognize that our vision of that future may be as limited as Gutenberg's must have been when he printed his first book.

Appendix: Excerpts from the Association of Viewdata Information Providers' Code of Practice

Preamble

1. Introduction

1.1   Viewdata is a system of transmitting alpha-numeric and graphic data along the existing Post Office telephone network, and displaying it on a television screen at the request of the user. The data may be stored in computers belonging to the Post Office (the present Prestel system) — or to anyone else (including the "user" himself) permitted to operate viewdata systems; and the data may be received in a number of other ways — including on tape, in direct print-out, or in telex form.

1.2   Within the law and relevant codes, the data can be on any subject whatever, and can be provided for storage by any Information Provider who has signed a contract with a viewdata system operator, (e.g. the Post Office in the case of Prestel), or any sub-information provider (see Appendix II).

1.3   Viewdata is not broadcasting —
nor is it "television"—
it is not printed —
nor is it "advertising" —
although it partakes of aspects of all of these.

In consequence, material placed on viewdata is in a special category not covered adequately by the well-established codes and regulations covering the existing media. It is therefore essential to draw up a Code of Practice which, while including the key aspects of these other codes, also allows for the special features of viewdata.

1.4   The special features of this new medium (which can be designated as "electronic publishing") are:-
  unlimited storage capacity
  permanent accessibility
  instant up-dating
  immediate access
  interactivity
  universal availability

1.5   Some of the consequences of these special features are:-
  (a)   The *unlimited capacity* and *instant updating* mean that it will, in practice, be impossible to monitor material before it goes on the database.
  (b)   The *permanent accessibility* means that material will stay on the database for as long as the IP wishes, and it is not ephemeral like TV, radio or the Press. On the other hand, using this medium will be a "calculated act of viewing" in that no change will take place on the screen unless the user presses a button (unlike TV where programmes continue to unfold unless stopped).
  (c)   *Immediate access* with *interactivity* means that it will be used in the home for (inter alia) the direct purchase of goods, by anyone in the house.
  (d)   *Universal availability* means that anyone may be able to see it at any time, in any part of the world.

1.6   The Council of AVIP accepts the need to update this Code of Practice continuously as the medium develops, and generally in advance of anything which
could be achieved by legislation. It will be glad to receive any suggestions from
any quarter, and undertakes to liaise with other professional or trade bodies
whose interests involve viewdata.

1.7   The principles of conduct governing the use of viewdata for gambling, lotteries
prize competitions, etc., will be defined later, but prior to their introduction on
the system. Current experience with this type of use of viewdata is nil.

2.   Principles
2.1   It is established as a basic principle that viewdata should be available to all
potential IPs (Information Providers), and that the range of data stored should
be as wide as possible — including the free expression of opinions.

2.2   All material stored must comply in every respect with the laws of the United
Kingdom both common and statute. A selected list of legislation relevant to
viewdata is at Appendix III of this section.

2.3   All Information Providers are to be encouraged to join the Trade Association
formed for this purpose — The Association of Viewdata Information Providers
Limited — whose members are bound by this Code of Practice.

2.4   The Association will provide a service (see Appendix I) for the receipt and investigation of complaints about material on the AVIP members' pages. Where a
complaint is upheld, the IP will be required to remove or amend the frame(s) in
question. Details of the complaints service will be available free on viewdata, as
well as from the Association.

2.5   The Code lays down criteria of professional conduct for AVIP member IPs and
provides the public with a clear indication of self-imposed limitations accepted
by those working on viewdata. It is accepted by IPs in the broad spirit as well as
the letter, and is therefore intended to set standards in a medium not yet defined
in law — the possibilities of which have scarcely begun to be understood. The
Code is intended to:-
        (a)   protect the interests of the user of viewdata
        (b)   set a high standard for the viewdata medium.

2.6   The Code of Practice covers all frames for which AVIP members are responsible, which are intended in any way to be accessible by the general public.

2.7   The security of any *confidential material* stored in viewdata systems is of major
importance. Arrangements must be worked out directly between IPs and
viewdata system operators (including the Post Office) to bar unauthorised access
on all occasions.

2.8   The Code embodies the essential principles of the British Code of Advertising
Practice, the IBA Code of Advertising Standards and Practice, and the Press
Council's Code. In addition, any IP who is a member of a Trade or Professional
Body is subject to the regulations of that body. Given the unique nature of the
viewdata medium, it was considered necessary to create a new Code of Practice
rather than cross-refer to an amalgam of existing codes.

Section 1
Information

1.   Introduction
1.1   AVIP considers that this section of the Code of Practice, as it relates to the quality of information being provided, is of the utmost importance for the well-being
and future of viewdata.

1.2   The prime purpose of viewdata is the communication of many types of information from suppliers of information (Information Providers) to persons requiring
that data. It is therefore essential that the quality of the material being provided
is of a consistently high standard. Main Information Providers (i.e. those
organisations which have a contract to lease pages from viewdata systems
operators such as the Post Office) are ultimately responsible for the quality of
the information stored and communicated via their pages, including all matter
provided by, for or with sub-information providers (see Appendix II of the
Preamble) and advertisers (see Section 2).

1.3 AVIP will defend the rights of any member Information Provider to provide any type of information on viewdata that complies with this Code of Practice. AVIP will contest attempts by any organisations to censor information being provided on viewdata as long as it conforms to this Code of Practice.

2. Principles Governing the Quality and Pricing of Information on Viewdata

2.1 The Information Provider shall not publish on viewdata any information which, or any part of which is grossly offensive or the publication transmission or use of which, or any part of which will be in breach of any statutory provision or the common law or an infringement of any private right, and shall ensure as respects the intended publication transmission or use of any information that all necessary licences, consents, permissions and authorisations have been obtained and all requirements of law have been complied with before such information is published on viewdata.

2.2 The name of the organisation or individual providing information (whether Information Provider or sub-information provider) should be clearly and unambiguously stated on each viewdata page.

2.3 The information published on viewdata should be presented clearly and unambiguously.

2.4 The information published on viewdata should not be designed to mislead.

2.5 The information published on viewdata should be accurate.

2.6 Where information on viewdata is of a topical nature it should be clearly dated and, if necessary, timed.

2.7 Distinctions between information and advertising (see beginning of Section 2) should be clearly drawn.

2.8 Completeness of Information

2.8.1 The information provided on a topic should aim to be as complete as is reasonably possible, (i.e. if it professes to cover train times, then a reasonable proportion of the likely train routes should be available).

2.8.2 Invalid routes should be avoided (i.e. cases where an advertised choice gives the response "SORRY NO SUCH PAGE").

2.8.3 On any page only a minority of routes should be blocked off by the standard ■.

2.9 Routing

2.9.1 Where the user is invited on a given page to move to a next page or pages either by keying 0-9 or by direct dialling using the * # facility, the information to be found on the next page or pages should be clearly if briefly stated on the given page. The user should in no circumstances be misled about the information he/she will find as a result of making a choice about the next page.

2.9.2 Where the user is invited on a given page to move to a next page or pages which are set at a different price to the given page, the change of price information should be clearly and unambiguously stated on the given page. Price changes should be signalled on the screen in close proximity to the choices offered (i.e. key 3 - 5p per frame).

2.9.3 Where the user is invited on a given page to move to a next page or pages which involve a change of Information Provider, or sub-information provider, the change of Information Provider should be clearly and unambiguously stated on the given page. An Information Provider should not route the user to the pages of another Information Provider without the latter's prior approval.

2.9.4 The use of double-digit keying (10, 11, 12, 13) is prohibited *unless* the full cost implications are explained to the user.

2.9.5 Information Providers promoting their pages in other media outside Prestel (e.g. directories) must state in those other media prices of pages which the user is being encouraged to call up.

2.9.6 In routing a user through a database, Information Providers must provide the route that is most economical to the user.

2.10 Pricing

The price of each page of information on viewdata must be clearly stated on the screen.

2.11 Response pages

The information on response pages should be clearly and unambiguously presented. Users must be in no doubt as to the consequence of using the 2-way facility (i.e. that their names and addresses, for example, are made available to the Information Provider).

2.12 Misuse of editing numbers

Any unauthorised changes, by any Information Provider or sub-information provider, to any other Information Provider's or sub-information provider's pages, by whatever means is strictly prohibited. All Information Providers or sub-information providers must ensure the highest security for any editing passwords which are issued to them.

Section 3
Direct Sale of Goods and Services

1.   General

1.1   In this section of the Code of Practice governing the direct sale of goods or services via viewdata using, for example, the two-day interactive capability:-

(a)   "Supplier" means a person who is undertaking to sell goods or supply services directly;

(b)   "Information Provider" means the person who has a contract with the viewdata system operator to supply frames of information;

(c)   "Consumer" means any person offering to buy goods or be supplied with services.

1.2   All goods and services advertised for direct sale on viewdata shall be treated as "invitations to treat" and "direct sale" shall be construed accordingly.

1.3   An offer to purchase goods or services advertised shall be made by the consumer by pressing the required keys on the response page and/or communicating with the supplier in other ways, according to the instructions given.

1.4   Every offer so made may be accepted or rejected by the supplier.

1.5   Every contract shall be capable of being evidenced in writing by the supplier.

1.6   Every advertisement for goods or services for direct sale shall contain the name of the supplier.

1.7   All suppliers shall be required to open a separate bank account into which all prepayments by consumers, whether deposits, part payments or the full price shall be paid. The supplier shall not draw any money from such account until the goods or services are delivered to the consumer. This paragraph shall not apply to prepayments using the frame price mechanism of response pages.

1.8   Every supplier undertakes that it will not advertise goods or services for direct sale unless there exists at the time of the advertisement sufficient stock to meet expected demand.

2.   Prices

2.1   All goods and services advertised for direct sale via viewdata shall have a clear and accurate indication of the cash price at which they are to be sold inclusive of VAT.

2.2   The advertised price must state separately, clearly and accurately any charge for delivery, postage and packing or other sum payable by the consumer.

2.3   In direct sale advertisements, no price shall be qualified by the use of the words "worth", "value", "as low as", "only".

2.4   The word "free" shall not be used in any advertisement where the consumer has to pay any sum of any kind to any person, other than telephone and connection charges.

2.5   Where with one purchase a consumer is offered in addition a "free" product, the supplier must be able to show to the Association that the consumer is not making any financial contribution to the cost of the "free" product.

2.6   All indications of credit terms for direct sale purchases must comply with Part 4 of this Section.

3.   Sale of Goods

3.1   All goods will be supplied on a sale or return basis.

3.2   Delivery of goods must be made within 28 days of the supplier accepting the consumer's offer.

3.3   If delivery is not made within that period, the supplier must notify the consumer in writing of the anticipated delivery date. On receipt of this notification, the consumer may cancel the contract by notice in writing and be refunded immediately with any money he has paid.

3.4   If the goods are damaged in transit:-
     (a)   The consumer may request the supplier to replace them within 14 days of notice of the damage; or
     (b)   The consumer may require the supplier to cancel the contract and make a full refund to the consumer; or
     (c)   If the goods are capable of repair, the consumer may request the supplier to arrange for such repair at no cost to the consumer and compensate the consumer for the loss of use of the goods.

3.5   Where goods are retained by a customer after the agreed approval period (which should not be less than 14 days), the supplier may send an invoice.

3.6   All goods will remain the property of, and at risk of, the supplier until they have been supplied to the consumer and he has retained them for the agreed approval period (which should not be less than 14 days).

3.7   Where goods do not correspond with any description and are not of merchantable quality or fit for the purpose for which they are intended, the supplier shall refund the price paid by the consumer together with all out-of-pocket expenses incurred by the consumer.

3.8   If goods are not available, a supplier may offer a consumer a close substitute, and will modify his advertisement on viewdata immediately. Such a close substitute will be subject to all provisions of this Code. The consumer may refuse such substitutes, receive a refund, and return them at no cost to the consumer.

3.9   (a)   No guarantees given with goods or services shall contain terms made void by Unfair Contract Terms Act 1977;
     (b)   All guarantees given with goods shall comply with the Consumer Transactions (Restrictions on Statements) Order 1976 (as amended);
     (c)   No guarantee shall be given in respect of goods comprised in contracts for services unless they are capable of being carried into effect.

3.10   Where advertised goods have to be assembled by the consumer, this fact shall be clearly stated in the advertisement.

3.11   All goods advertised shall comply with:-
     (a)   Any relevant British Standard or other approved Standard;
     (b)   Regulations made under the Consumer Protection Act 1961;
     (c)   Regulations made under the Consumer Safety Act 1978.

4.   Credit

4.1   All advertising of credit facilities in relation to direct sale purchases shall comply with:-
     (a)   The Advertisements (Hire Purchase) Act 1967;
     (b)   The Consumer Credit Act 1974.

4.2   No disclosure of any financial information obtained by the supplier shall be made to any one apart from the consumer himself unless he consents in writing after being supplied with the information.

4.3   Suppliers shall abide by the terms of the agreements entered into with the various credit card companies.

4.4   The provisions of the Consumer Credit Act 1974 relating to the form and contents of documents used for credit transactions shall apply to all credit agreements made by the supplier when the regulations come into force.

4.5   In all advertisements in which credit prices are quoted, the Annual Percentage Rate of Charge shall appear in clear and accurate type.

5.   Conclusion

5.1   In any advertisement for the direct sale of goods or supply of services aimed at children, suppliers will have regard for safety both of products and of the conditons under which they might be used.

5.2   Except as otherwise provided by this Section, the direct sale of goods and services by viewdata and its accompanying advertisements are governed by the other relevant paragraphs of this Code of Practice.

LIST OF ACRONYMS

ANSI   American National Standards Institute

AT&T   American Telephone & Telegraph

CBS   Columbia Broadcasting Service

CCITT   The Consultative Committee on International Telephony and Telegraphy

DBS   Direct Satellite-to-home Broadcasting

DRCS   Dynamically Redefinable Character Sets

EIA   Electronic Industries Association

FBS   First Bank System, Inc.

FCC   Federal Communications Commission

ITU   International Telecommunications Union

MDS   Multipoint Distribution Service

SCA   Subsidiary Communication Authorization

VBI   Vertical Blanking Interval

Index

141

About the Author

Richard M. Neustadt is a communications lawyer in the Washington, DC office of Kirkland & Ellis. He handles legislative, regulatory and business development matters for clients involved in communications and computer hardware, transmission and content.

Mr. Neustadt is a graduate of Harvard College and Harvard Law School. After service in the U.S. Navy, he worked as a news writer for CBS News. From 1977 until 1981 he was Associate Director of the White House Domestic Policy staff. He advised President Carter and coordinated Administration activities in the area of regulatory reform including communications, transportation and overall regulatory procedures. Since leaving the White House at the end of the Carter Administration, Mr. Neustadt has written and spoken extensively on communications policy issues affecting electronic publishing and home transactions services. He is also a founding member of the Videotex Industry Association and serves on several of its policy committees.

Related Titles From Knowledge Industry Publications, Inc. . .

The Business of Consumer Magazines
by Benjamin M. Compaine
LC 82-180   ISBN 0-86729-020-X   hardcover $32.95

The Future of Videotext
by Efrem Sigel et al.
                        ISBN 0-86729-025-0   hardcover $32.95

Viewdata and Videotext, 1980-81: A Worldwide Report
LC 80-18234   ISBN 0-914236-77-6   softcover $75.00

Electronic Document Delivery: The Artemis Concept
by Adrian Norman
LC 81-20774   ISBN 0-86729-011-0   hardcover $45.00

U.S. Book Publishing Yearbook and Directory, 1981-1982
edited by Judith Duke
LC 79-649219   ISBN 0-914236-63-6   softcover $60.00

Guide to Electronic Publishing: Opportunities in Online and Viewdata Services
by Fran Spigai and Peter Sommer
LC 81-12319   ISBN 0-914236-87-3   softcover $95.00

The Print Publisher in an Electronic World
LC 81-671   ISBN 0-914236-81-4   softcover $95.00

Video Discs: The Technology, The Applications and The Future
by Efrem Sigel, Mark Schubin, Paul F. Merril, et al.
LC 79-18797   ISBN 0-914236-56-3   hardcover $29.95

Books, Libraries and Electronics: Essays on the Future of Communication
by Efrem Sigel, Lewis Branscomb, Dan Lacy, et al.
LC 82-15229   ISBN 0-86729-024-2   hardcover $24.95

Knowledge Industry Publications, Inc.
White Plains, NY 10604